IDENTITY MATTERS

God, I will give thanks to You and praise Your name! All glory, honor, and power are Yours! Because my life is Yours, help me present myself as someone who belongs to You! Let my whole life bring You glory! In Jesus' name, Amen.

IDENTITY MATTERS

The Power of

Jeff Frick

Library of Congress Catalog Number: 2023946657

First Printing: November 2023
23 24 25 26 27 28   10 9 8 7 6 5 4 3 2 1

Praise for: IDENTITY MATTERS

"Belonging serves as a barometer of our lives. Our identities inherently emerge from the answers to questions where do I belong and to whom do I belong to? Questions that we all encounter at various points of our lives. Questions that, for many of us, persistently plague our lives.

There are some books that are written for a contemporary cultural moment, and others written as a transcendent treasure. Pastor Jeff Frick, a dear friend, has contributed mightily to the latter. 'Identity Matters: The Power of Belonging' is a book that will remain relevant and needed despite whatever cultural whims we face. It is deeply intimate, as Jeff beautifully weaves his life experiences throughout. While universally relatable, as I read his many personal stories, I began to recall similar incidents in my own journey. He helped me see things I had previously missed.

The story of the Bible, and the story of our lives, are often buttressed by these twin pillars of belonging and division. Sin divided us from God, yet Jesus reconciled us on the cross, so we belong again to Him. In our lives, we often encounter pain and suffering marked by division of some sort. While love and hope are often tethered to belonging. The beauty of this book is that Jeff discusses so many aspects of our lives that relate to division, but he helps us see how in those moments, harnessing the answers to questions like where do I belong and to whom do I belong to, will lead to true belonging. Belonging to Jesus Christ.

As the world pulls us apart, Pastor Jeff Frick instructs and encourages us that belonging will keep us together. Belonging properly situated in Christ. This is a must read, a necessary read!"

Rev. Brandon Cleaver,
Director of the Matthew 5:9 Fellowship

"'Identity Matters: The Power of Belonging' is a raw book that author Jeff Frick inserts the reader into each story, making it feel as if you're standing right next to him. The vulnerability and emotion of this testimonial story, makes it a must read for all. I recommend this book to anyone who is searching for belonging. The word belong, has different meanings depending on how you were raised and what you believe. This book takes the reader on a journey of reflection and provides a platform to understand what belonging means to them. Each chapter of the book eloquently gives the reader thoughts and lessons to ponder while reading. You will be changed after reading this book. More importantly, you will know you belong to Christ Jesus."

Brandon Jezdimir, Principal
Notre Dame Prep Middle School

"Jeff Frick provides a wealth of wisdom, obtained through his diligent observations, alert curiosity, and a willingness to engage others to gain insights and reveal truth. He meets people where they are, and with an unoffendable heart, helps them to explore and discover the exciting experience of a redemptive relationship with Jesus, through obedience to our Father. Jeff demonstrates Christlike behavior, without obstructing the view, so that all we can see is God's glory. He asks questions and shares raw stories that challenge, nurture, heal, refine, and inspire us to consider new perspectives, and grow into more loving, joyous, and peaceful servants.

Whose are we? Why are we here? Where do we belong? What are we doing? How do choices affect others? What is community and how are relationships created? Find out how 'Identity Matters: The Power of Belonging' can help you to define your identity, shape your purpose, elevate your spirit, restore your life, and experience belonging!"

"Dr. Phil" Andrews
Author "Sally & Sam Squirrel, and The Oak Tree Forest"

"I have had the pleasure and honor of knowing Jeff Frick for a few years now. I count him as a friend and brother in Christ. He has been an incredible mentor to me, and I love our sharpening sessions. I now feel that I know Jeff at a much deeper level. Through the raw retelling of his many stories, he took me back through my own life looking through the lens of belonging. There were many themes that stood out as Jeff took me on this journey. The power of vulnerability and how this can create a space for others to open up and receive truth in love. This is such a key aspect of building trust and allowing others to be vulnerable too, so we know their story. Through learning the stories of others, we can now see the collateral damage of generational sin as well as the self-destructing ways we sabotage ourselves in response to our own pain. Jeff really creates a blueprint for helping others to break the cycle and become redeemed through the power of a relationship with Jesus Christ. It all starts with belonging and knowing who we are and Whose we are. Our purpose can come from our pain if we see others as Jesus sees them. Not as problems to be fixed, but people to be loved with no judgment. Jeff has taught me that once we have belonging, we now can believe and become who God has called us into being. Let's go!"

Tim Morton, Fellowship of Christian Athletes
SE Michigan Area Director

"This is a rare book that gives a reminder of how much we long to belong together, as one family under God in community. You will find this book profoundly honest and uplifting as it provides hope of how we can heal our wounds that stem from searching in the wrong places. Pastor Jeff Frick explains through real life experiences how Jesus heals our broken hearts from all the false idols in our lives when we belong to and allow Christ to reign over all our affections. Through an identity firmly rooted in Jesus, we learn to offer grace, mercy, forgiveness, healing, and hospitality to one another as we grow in our belonging to Him."

Bob Pyle, Pastor of Salem Brethren Church
Mt. Pleasant Mills, PA

"Deep within our souls exists a burning desire to belong and the fever from this desire creates a thirst that we set out to quench. Jeff captures this innate longing and takes us on a journey of discovery for belonging. He identifies the traps and perils of seeking to fulfill this thirst from the wrong sources and then leads us to the true source that can not only fulfill our need but also supply us enough to share and lead others. In a rich and very real way, Jeff shares his personal story riddled with pain and struggles along the way of discovery.

You will not read this book as a bystander but will find yourself somewhere within its pages, somewhere deep within the story, somewhere within the struggles, but will ultimately discover the joy of knowing you belong, and the responsibility birthed from that position of awareness. In an inspiring way, you will discover what God allows to come your way and whatever He brings you to, He will also bring you through with a greater sense of who you are and Whose you are. Jeff reveals that God takes your brokenness and through his amazing grace, will orchestrate what you are becoming and solidify your sense of belonging! Thank you Jeff and praise God for this work."

Donearl Johnson, Lead Pastor of Life Church
Auburn Hills, MI

Dedication

This book is dedicated to my awe-inspiring, newly born, grandson Jackson.

Jackson, you will bring more joy into this world than you could possibly imagine. So many lives will be inspired because of your very existence. The love that will be cascaded on you will rival the greatest waterfall. You will emanate a light that will never diminish. We are excited to watch you grow, Jackson, our first grandchild!

While your father and I were preparing your nursery, we were discussing all the tasks that had yet to be completed to finish your room. I reminded your father that soon he would know what it would be like to hold you in his arms. In that moment, and forever more, there would be nothing that he wouldn't do for you. In fact, there is nothing both your parents wouldn't do for you, they love you!

Your grandmother and I can't wait to spoil you. We love you dearly!
Blessings,

Grandpa

Numbers 6:24-26 (NIV), "The Lord bless you and keep you; the Lord make his face shine on you and be gracious to you; the Lord turn his face toward you and give you peace."

Table of Contents

Foreword

Everyone wants to be seen, not just observed, but welcomed into the other person's life as a valuable member. This statement made by Jeff, during one of our many times together, shows that he has a unique ability to articulate this idea of wanting to be known rather than just looked at or merely known about.

Jeff has a wealth of experience from which he draws his life examples to help us understand the value that relationships have. He helps us have an increasing desire to do the work of eliminating anything that will interfere with our *belonging* to God and others.

You'll see in this book how valuable each person is, and that they have been given a uniqueness from infancy to adulthood from God.

I highly recommend this book to you.

Loren Siffring M.D., Pastor, friend

Jeff Frick

Acknowledgements

I have many people to thank for helping me in the writing of this book. I was inspired by a revelation from the Lord God to write my first book. God nudged me to write this book as well. It's pretty amazing that I have now written two books and have never had a personal interest, thought, or goal to write one. God is so incredible!

Many have helped with the most difficult process of editing this book and I would like to thank them. This list is quite lengthy, but each of them deserves my gratitude for the countless hours in reading and re-reading this book. Once again, a special thank you goes out to Judy Daggett. She led the charge in the editing process. The names listed below made it possible for you, the reader, to receive the best achievable product.

Thank you Barry Nannini!
Thank you Loren Siffring!
Thank you Tim Morton!
Thank you Dave Green!
Thank you Dave Torres!
Thank you Chris Bokmuller!
Thank you Judy Daggett!
Thank you Maria DeKimpe!
Thank you Ron Daggett!
Thank you Tim Renaud!
Thank you Allison Renaud!
Thank you Andy Kelly!
Thank you Mike Lock!
Thank you Matteo McGill!
Thank you Julia Brunicardi!
Thank you James Frick!
Thank you Bob Frick!

Because of all of you, this book is available to readers.

1 Thessalonians 1:2 (NIV), "We always thank God for all of you and continually mention you in our prayers."

Author's Note

I want to make sure that the readers of this book know that the contents found within are *"my"* perspective of the events in my life that brought me to enlightenment. Some of the stories you will read are quite piercing and rather revealing. As a result, many may be offended by the words. I want to assure everyone that this book was not written to harm anyone, but to help those who may be caught in the world of confusion and not living in the redemption of Christ. The stories written within represent only a microcosm of my life. Unfortunately, when you are searching to understand and no one around you can provide the answers, moments can seem like an eternity. I started searching for answers early in my childhood, continued as a young adult, and have never stopped. The people mentioned in the stories are no different than you or I. Every person comes to enlightenment in different ways and at different times. None of us wake up in the morning with the intention of hurting another person, but every day we say or do something unkind without realizing it.

One of the biggest obstacles we all face on any given day, and in any area of our lives, is the willingness to continue to grow and learn. Many of us get to a point in life where we feel comfortable with the way we see the world and we set up camp deciding this is how we will live our lives. This resting place becomes the vantage point from which we test, view, and approve every circumstance moving forward unless we are willing to continue to learn and grow. Unfortunately, if we are those who have rested, we have already placed our flag in the ground and anyone who thinks, talks, or acts differently than we do, is usually subject to our staunch scrutiny. This undoubtedly births conflict. This occurs because we, those who have rested, have decided that there is no other way than our way. There are two areas of life where humanity does not excel: communicating clearly and solving conflict. Our conflicts continue to mount mostly because we don't value our relationships more than we value ourselves. Self-protection always places the relationship at a far distant second.

Those who have rested, tend to find their identity in something that is less than the truth. This means they are not set free and always feel the need to protect themselves when their identity is threatened by a different point of view. This does not mean they are a bad person. Every person has blind spots and must continually fight to remove them. It's only when we have rested and refuse to move from our vantage point that we find difficulty without end. We attempt to solve people's problems through our eyes and not through those we are in relationship with. We fail to see others point of view. We also tend to decide when people should be able to move on and forget the conflict that we don't know how to solve. We do this, I want to emphasize, because we have *decided* that there is no other way than *our* way.

Now, imagine being a child and living in this space with parents who have made the choice to divorce. Not only have they complicated their lives, but they have also complicated their children's lives as well. They have not figured out how to see things from other people's perspective because they can rarely resolve their own thoughts. Thus, the conflict continues to grow. How long would it take for the child to grow beyond all the confusion and begin to mature to see things from a healthy perspective? When will this child find **belonging**? This book *is* that story. It's my perspective, my journey. It's also important to note that if I had not found God along the way, I would most likely still be lost in the brokenness. Without God we are constantly searching to fill the void that was, is, and always will be reserved for Him. Perhaps you can now begin to see the endless cycle we find ourselves in?

> *1 Peter 2:9 (NIV), "But you are a chosen people, a royal priesthood, a holy nation, God's special possession, that you may declare the praises of him who called you out of darkness into his wonderful light."*

Again, I want to reiterate, this book and the stories herein, are not meant to discredit, hurt, or harm anyone. I only hope to help those who are caught in a place of confusion and conflict and don't know how to escape. There is a growing concern for peace and unity in our world. There are many people who have no **belonging**. Every attempt to be a peacemaker must be explored. Every attempt to bring unity in division must not be overlooked. Only those who have **belonging** can bring **belonging** to those who lack **belonging**. I was faced with many obstacles in the writing of this book, and prayerfully believe that it was God's prompting that brought this book forward. He asked me to write it for the benefit of others. God has leveraged every difficult moment of my life to bring glory to His Name, to bring healing to those who are hurting, to free those who are lost, and to teach people the value of *belonging*. I am confident you will be blessed by reading it.

Psalm 100:3 (TPT), "....we have the privilege of worshiping Yahweh our God. For he is our Creator and we belong to him. We are the people of his pleasure."

1

What is Belonging?

John 1:12 (NIV), "Yet to all who did receive him, to those who believed in his name, he gave the right to become children of God."

Have you ever been in the middle of a group of people but somehow still felt alone? Maybe that group was a crowd of strangers or casual acquaintances in the workplace, perhaps even family members in your own home. Just because you're surrounded doesn't mean you always feel connected, or that you fit in. We are social creatures and long to fit in. Perhaps our society's dismantling of biblical principles has brought us to a place where we no longer know how to be "with" people. If that is true, and there is certainly overwhelming evidence to support that theory, considering our self-willed and self-attained morals, our fragmented or tribal social groups, along with technology and the destruction of the family unit, then where do we turn and where do we go to find *belonging*? If the majority of people can't provide this necessary component of fellowship and community, largely because it has remained elusive to them, how would we begin to restore it in ourselves so that we can begin to share it once again? The short answer is Jesus Christ.

A close look at the Bible reveals that these social groups exist because God made us that way. He made us to live in relationship—to *belong*—and God has a purpose for that *belonging*. Jesus offers a connection and a *belonging* that works from the inside out. In fact, once He comes into your heart and saturates your life, you will never have to be separated or alone again. We can backslide, but when you turn back to Jesus, He will always provide and strengthen your *belonging*. God made us for relationships. We were built to *belong*, and any form of fragmented isolation actually works against how God has designed us to live.

As you read this book, my hope is that you begin to realize the power that ***belonging*** has on us. My purpose for writing this book is to share my experience(s) in the search of my ***belonging***. Each person has been bestowed with an innate sense to ***belong***. Ultimately, my search led me to Jesus, but along the way, I learned many valuable lessons. ***Belonging*** that comes from the wrong place, will never truly quench our thirst. Believe it or not, ***belonging*** that only offers pretentiousness, of which there are many sources, will always leave us wanting, never fulfilled. When we finally succumb to the fact that the world, and the people who inhabit it, can only provide a sliver of true ***belonging***, we may ask ourselves why it took so long for us to figure it out.

The foundation, or beginning, of our understanding of ***belonging*** starts with the family. Regrettably, the darkness of our world is breaking that ***belonging*** down, *destroying* the family and the birth of ***belonging***. My journey was long because of the dynamics of my broken family. You will read some of those specifics in later chapters. One thing is certain, we should recognize and appreciate that every moment we experienced on this journey, waiting to come to the truth, was not only necessary, but also provided what was essential for us to be able to share the truth about ***belonging*** more effectively.

Below is a list of questions that you should find answers to as you progress through the book.

1. What is ***belonging***?

2. Where do I ***belong***?

3. Can we escape from the power of wanting to ***belong***?

4. Can the desire to ***belong*** be fulfilled?

5. Why do we search for ***belonging*** in the wrong places?

6. When we find ***belonging***, especially after a long search, why are we willing to push others away and keep them from the same desire?

7. How do we love others who cannot give us ***belonging*** or don't know how?

8. Why is ***belonging*** attached to our identity?

Before we can understand what ***belonging*** is, we must initially answer the questions, "Where do I ***belong***?" And, "Who do I ***belong*** to?" According to the Scriptures, we ***belong*** to God, who is our Creator, and we ***belong*** to, and are each a part of the body of Christ who holds all things together.

> *Romans 12:4-5 (NIV), "For just as each of us has one body with many members, and these members do not all have the same function, so in Christ we, though many, form one body, and each member **belongs** to all the others."*

> *Colossians 1:15-17 (NIV), "The Son is the image of the invisible God, the firstborn over all creation. For in him all things were created: things in heaven and on earth, visible and invisible, whether thrones or powers or rulers or authorities; all things have been created through him and for him. He is before all things, and in him all things hold together."*

We must also understand that ***belonging*** is not a destination we arrive at. Our ***belonging*** can be continually fortified, strengthened, and deepened as we grow in understanding and maturity. However, we will never find a fulfilling sense of ***belonging*** until we are firmly rooted in the assurance of "who" we are and "Whose" we are. For many of us, our identity in Jesus, who He says we are, isn't always easy to accept. Many fight their way through life comparing themselves with others because they don't understand how valuable they truly are. But once you embrace the truth of who you are, you won't strive to prove it to anyone. You will be at peace with who you are and be happy with how God made you. As the passage from Romans, Chapter 12, previously shared above, alludes to, we each have a different function, or a gifting. For our ***belonging*** to become firmly rooted in us, we must understand our gifting, our contribution to the kingdom of God. Knowing that we contribute in a unique and specific way, allows us to be as independent as we are interdependent. In other words, when we know "who" we are and "Whose" we are, we can walk in our gifting separately, if needed. We can stand on our own but recognize the value of being together. We don't necessarily *need* each other, but we desire to be *with* each other.

Another element that is crucial to the reinforcing of our **belonging** is a feeling of happiness that goes beyond an immediate gratification based on something external. It is a happiness that extends beyond finding satisfaction in comparing oneself to another, such as in the competition of having more, one that provides a feeling of fulfillment. Deep seated **belonging** requires a contributive happiness, one where we are excited by seeing the good in others and doing good for others. If we see or perceive that another person is gaining something, then our contribution to the purpose is increased. At this level of happiness, we are not wanting to find other's weaknesses but are looking to love them and encourage them to make things better. There is a challenge we apply here, not to be over someone but to encourage them to do better, be quicker, or perform more efficiently. When we learn to challenge others and at the same time be receptive to receive challenge from others, **belonging** grows. We can then share in the deposit of something valuable, together. Being loyal to each other or to our specific group will not provide **belonging**. However, loyalty with a purpose can continually move us to greater happiness and fulfillment.

In the first chapter of Genesis, we read the words, "Let there be" spoken by God over and over. These are creative word(s). Later in Genesis, we also read "let us" which is another form of creation.

Genesis 1:26-27 (NIV), 'Then God said, "Let us make mankind in our image, in our likeness, so that they may rule over the fish in the sea and the birds in the sky, over the livestock and all the wild animals, and over all the creatures that move along the ground." So God created mankind in his own image, in the image of God he created them; male and female he created them.'

In the verses above, mankind was created and given purpose. If we (humans) are continually involved in creation, then purpose is evidence of our **belonging**. Taken another step further, in "let us" we find the Triune God; Father, Son and Holy Spirit asking us to do what they did. The Father imagines it, the Son puts it into words, and the Holy Spirit applies it. What was created **belongs** to all three of them with different functions but the same purpose. So, when two or more of us agree to a purpose, a time, and to use our unique functions, we can involve each other in a decision to create something that wasn't there before. Then what is created ***belongs*** to those who were a part of the creation. As we are created in God's image, we are to mimic our Creator in making something with a common purpose, together. Thus, the desire to want to ***belong*** is also part of our creative nature.

Hebrews tells us that Jesus even identified with us in temptation so we could ***belong*** to Him. How wonderful to know that our Heavenly Father went to such great lengths to provide every assurance necessary for us to receive the fulfillment of knowing that we ***belong*** to Him. In our best days and in our weakest days, Jesus can identify with us.

Hebrews 4:15 (NIV), "For we do not have a high priest who is unable to empathize with our weaknesses, but we have one who has been tempted in every way, just as we are—yet he did not sin."

So, what is ***belonging***? ***Belonging*** is the innate desire to be connected to, or part of, something that brings fulfillment and happiness. ***Belonging*** comes from our Heavenly Father, the assurance that we have a purpose, that we fit in, that we are accepted, that we are loved. We need the experience of a continually developing connection to social and family groups where we can contribute to something greater than ourselves. We will always search for and long for ***belonging***.

Resist

James 4:7, (NIV), "Submit yourselves, then, to God. Resist the devil, and he will flee from you."

In the course of writing this book, a series of events unfolded which almost caused me to discontinue completing the book forever. In the writing of my first book, I secured 14 friends to help with the editing process. Similarly, while writing this book, I asked 17 friends to help with the editing process. The more eyes that scrutinize the book, the better the result for the eventual reader. When one of those friends began to share the results of their first look at the book, something far-reaching took place. This person suggested that I remove the two chapters (4 and 5) from the book that pertain to my family because there was nothing redeeming attached to them. My first thought to this suggestion was that I didn't know how I would be able to fill the void.

This book is not an informational book about **belonging**. This book is my journey of learning what **belonging** is and from Whom the depth of **belonging** comes from. This book represents the journey of my discovery in finding **belonging**. If this was indeed to be an informational book about **belonging**, I would need to include elements of race, culture, and gender to name a few to make it complete. That was not the book that I believed God wanted me to write. In fact, God gave me the title to this book almost a year earlier. I know that some of the stories in the chapters containing my family are very hard to read. My goal is neither to harm anyone, nor to shame anyone, or is it to make fun of anyone. Today I am grateful for the things that have happened in my life. God has leveraged all of them to bring glory to His name, and to bring awareness and healing to myself and countless others. However, the fact remains that these stories did happen, and they are part of my journey to discover **belonging**. Additionally, because of the brokenness in the world, both in and out of the church, redemption does not always occur. This is because we must learn to allow God into our lives. Too many people are unwilling to do so.

After hearing the suggestion to remove the chapters, I paused writing and set out to hear from God as to whether I should write the book or not. I also sought counsel from many of the others who were helping with the editing process. Most of those whom I asked encouraged me to seek the Lord in prayer. I prayed many times that God would lead me to the answer. I went to my evening Bible study group and my friend Matt noticed that I was deep in thought. He said, "You have something big on your mind, it's written all over your face. Care to talk about it?" I shared my concerns with him. I told him what happened when I sent the chapters to my brother.

I stated, "While my brother was printing the pages at his office, he had to step away for a phone call. When my brother returned, he found one of his employees reading one of the pages. The employee looked at my brother and said, 'Who is this about? If I didn't know any better, I would say this is my life!' My brother called me and told me that this subject was bigger than I had previously realized."

After hearing this story, Matt said, "I would consider going in that direction. That might be a sign." Matt considered the conversation with my brother to be a clear indication that God was directing me to write the book.

Matt asked a lot of other questions and then he asked this, "Are you sure the original comment isn't from Satan? He always uses those closest to us to cause the greatest harm."

To which I replied, "I am not sure what to think at this point. Thanks for listening."

The next evening, I received a message from a pastor at my church. He asked if I could reach out to a man who was asking for help. I did manage to contact the man asking for help later that night. He asked if we could speak the next morning when he had more time and more privacy. I obliged him. After listening to the man's problems and concerns, my attention was immediately brought back to the book. This man had many family troubles, and he was both confused on how to proceed and felt ill-prepared to be able to make sense of how to tackle his circumstances. I began to think maybe God was trying to tell me to write the book as many people are struggling with how to build and maintain healthy families, solve conflict, communicate effectively, and find ***belonging***. Later that day I had a lunch date with a friend of mine. When I arrived at the restaurant, my friend asked how I was doing. I briefly told him that I was struggling to figure out if I was to write a book or not. I said that I needed God to share the direction in which I should go. I told him that I believed God was attempting to direct my path back to writing the book. I believed this, especially after the conversation I had earlier that day with the man looking for help.

As my friend and I sat down at our table, he asked, "What is the title of your book?"

I said, "Identity Matters: The Power of ***Belonging***."

My friend said, "That is so weird! I asked you to have lunch with me so I could ask you to help me understand how I can know for sure that I ***belong*** to God. I keep hearing voices that say I am not enough." Of course, I went right back to the thought that God was speaking to me. My friend and I had quite a long discussion about ***belonging*** and the values of walking with the Lord. After we finished our lunch, my friend went to the restroom, and I waited for him at the front door. While I was waiting for him, I pulled out my phone to check my messages. I am not a person who likes to see the red dot notifications next to the apps on my phone telling me something new is waiting. As soon as I see them, I perform whatever task is necessary to remove them. Maybe that makes me odd?

When I entered one of the apps, there was a message from a person that I had not been in contact with in over 15 years. The app made mention that it was the person's very first message under this particular platform. It was then that God had my full attention. You see, this person referenced in the app is the same person who asked me to drive a man to the hospital in the story found a little further in this chapter of this book, titled "Removal." More importantly, I had just entered that story into this book days prior to these events. When my friend returned, I said, "God just showed up again." He was ecstatic and so was I.

As I was driving home from lunch, I began to ponder, asking, "God, am I standing on the roof in the flood waiting for you to rescue me? You sent the rowboat, the raft, and the helicopter but I didn't notice because I am waiting for You." It was crystal clear that I **belong** to God, and He did tell me to write the book. Hallelujah! Sometimes we can become sidetracked and lose our focus. Satan will always attempt to come between you and God. Let us resist him and he will flee. I was interrupted, and God made it clear again in just two and one-half days.

Rejection

Acts 20:28 (NIV), "Keep watch over yourselves and all the flock of which the Holy Spirit has made you overseers. Be shepherds of the church of God, which he bought with his own blood."

I remember a man who once attended our Tuesday morning men's Bible study. He studied with us for nearly two years. This man was not a member of our congregation, but still he found his way to become part of our group. He attended a church that apparently was lacking a men's Bible study. Week after week, the man became increasingly more comfortable among us. This was wonderful to see, because it meant that our group had an inviting and accepting nature, even if we did not always display it. It wasn't long before the man grew more vocal and willing to share his thoughts and opinions, until he was fully integrated as part of the group. The man felt free to express himself and appeared by all accounts to feel welcomed, appreciated, and loved. We knew this because he was often waiting in the parking lot at 6 a.m. for the leader to arrive for the 6:30 study. Additionally, the man was more than willing to read his part and contribute to the weekly study. Each man would usually read 8-10 verses and then participate in the follow-up questions pertaining to the study.

Thus far, none of this story sounds extraordinary. A bunch of men who claim to follow Jesus, welcoming a man from a different church, recognizing that we are all One Body. That is until you find out that the man in the story has a speech impediment, a stutter. A stutter that prevented him from completing even a single sentence without the greatest of difficulty. To listen to the man communicate verbally was almost painful. Watching a man struggle syllable after syllable brought with it thoughts of how challenging it must have been for him growing up, especially considering the cruelty of children. I wondered how difficult it was, even in the present, for this man to brave the unkindness of adults? Spending time listening to him reminded me of Mel Tillis, a country music singer who also had a stutter. The difference between this man and Mel? This man's stutter would not disappear when he performed.

How does this story necessarily bring understanding and consciousness to the value of ***belonging*** to you, the reader? Throughout the year, the church which hosted the Bible study would organize volunteer recruitment weekends. These events were designed to create awareness of the various groups within the church and make them available for the congregants to join. The men in the Bible study would sometimes wonder why their group didn't consistently expand. When I shared the news that the volunteer recruitment weekend was quickly approaching, most of the men of the Bible study were excited. However, one person was not.

Over the next several weeks, the man referred to in the story became agitated, angry, disruptive, argumentative, and even malicious. Each week brought new levels of this behavior. Finally, many of the men approached the leader and said that they believed the man with the stutter should be removed from the group. His behavior was not improving, and he seemed to get more aggressive when anyone tried to talk to him about it. When all the complaints were heard, the leader shared something that was previously absent from the men's thoughts. The leader stated, "Imagine being a man who lived nearly 50 years in the prison of ill speech, surrounded by people who could not and/or would not concern themselves. Imagine the rare and fleeting moments when someone didn't treat him as odd or weird, almost like he was a leper (rejected, ostracized, outcast). Imagine a man who struggles immensely to verbally express himself in any meaningful way, who has learned to hibernate and separate from society."

The leader continued, "The man who had suffered all these experiences, and untold more, was now sitting at our table. Not just any random table, but a table of Christ followers deepening their understanding of the character of God. This man had grown to find peace, comfort, acceptance, love, and most of all *belonging*, among them. But now, in just a few short days, the fear of adding even one additional man to the group, let alone five or eight, would be enough to birth a fear in him. A fear so great that he believed he was about to lose his *belonging*. So, here we are witnessing a man who would go to great lengths in an attempt to preserve and protect what he has found. He is acting out-of-sorts because, maybe once again, he will have to retreat in deep anguish to a place of solitude, cocooning himself from the fear and pain of rejection."

When a new, and more than probable, vantage point of reality was shared with the men of the Bible study, they quickly changed their posture. Seeing, experiencing, and then finally understanding why the man with a stutter would change his behavior so abruptly brought enlightenment where there had once been blindness. It's a glaring reminder that there is always something to learn and always new ways to expand our love. Spending time with a man like this would prove that. The man eventually regained his composure and returned to his old self, especially when little change was made to our group. Sadly, the in-person restrictions brought about by COVID-19 would eventually cause him to leave the group as he was not a fan of video conferencing. It probably brought new fears that he had yet to experience in his life. For a man like him, who faced more than his fair share of challenges in the pursuit of *belonging*, he would not let himself be exposed to another loss. This story is just a single instance, in an endless sea of examples, of the power of **belonging** and what lengths a person would go to both find it and keep it.

Removal

Psalm 27:10 (NIV), "Though my father and mother forsake me, the Lord will receive me."

I have a friend who is an administrator for a law firm. The firm was responsible for planning and executing the needs of people who no longer could provide services for themselves. One of the main services they provided was the scheduling of doctor appointments, and transportation to and from. Another primary service was to make sure that groceries were delivered. The people they served had various disabilities, health problems, and unconventional circumstances. My friend Diane asked if I would be willing to pick up a man and take him to his outpatient surgery, wait for him, and then return him home. I agreed. When I arrived at his apartment complex, there was no mistaking that his place was extremely small. After he opened the door and introduced himself, it was apparent that this man had been in some serious accident. His ability to communicate, his mannerism, and his walking gait were noticeably unnatural.

As we were driving toward the hospital, I asked the man to tell me his story. "Tell me what happened to you that required a lawyer to have to step in and make your appointments for you," I inquired. At first, he didn't seem to want to share, but then he let his guard down. When he began to talk, he had a joyous light about him. He appeared to want to share how far he had progressed. His story was beyond anything that I had ever heard.

He said, "I used to own a roofing company and my girlfriend would help me with the bookkeeping. I always had lots of money and the work was always plentiful. Life was great! One day I fell off the roof of a two-story home. When I landed, I was somehow able to get right back up. Very quickly though, I started to feel sick, weak, and rundown. I knew something was wrong, so I went home." My girlfriend looked at me and said, "You are white as a ghost. Are you alright? I think we should take you to the hospital." The emergency room medical staff told my girlfriend that if I had gone to sleep,

I would have died. My brain was hemorrhaging, and they needed to operate to reduce the swelling, immediately.

He went on, "While I was in surgery to open my skull, I went into a coma. There I stayed for almost five years. After I woke up, I spent another two years in a rehabilitation center learning to walk again. I have been in my own apartment now for just over six months and there are still so many things that I am unable to do. However, I cannot tell you how wonderful and liberating it is to be living free. I am on my own and I don't need constant care. I am so happy."

I asked him about his family because he had been through quite an ordeal. He said, "Everyone has either left me or they have forgotten me. I look weird. I talk weird. I walk weird. Nobody wants to be around me. So, I am all by myself." Still, he had so much joy despite his circumstances. So much so, that I began to take inventory of my life to make sure that I was grateful. We arrived at the hospital, and I waited for him to be finished. On the way home he was very groggy from the anesthesia. We arrived back at his apartment, and I decided that I should walk him not just to his door but also go in and make sure he would be all right. When I got him settled, I noticed there was a picture of a little girl on top of the television set.

I asked, "Who is this little girl?"

He said, "That is my daughter."

I exclaimed, "Your daughter? You never mentioned her."

The man stated, "When I had my accident, my girlfriend was pregnant, but I did not know. She gave birth when I was in the coma. My daughter wants nothing to do with me just like everyone else."

At this, I wished him well and said, "Good-bye."

On the way home, I started to ponder, "Who do you **belong** to when everyone leaves you? How could it be that this man is full of joy even though his circumstances are dire?" Let us all be grateful for the things we have and for the people we share our life with, because one day you might meet someone who has the most unique and insane story that you have ever heard. A story where a person's **belonging** was cruelly and unjustly removed.

Praiseworthy

Philippians 4:8 (NIV), "Finally, brothers and sisters, whatever is true, whatever is noble, whatever is right, whatever is pure, whatever is lovely, whatever is admirable—if anything is excellent or praiseworthy—think about such things."

Sometimes it's hard to see the wonders that God is performing right in front of our eyes. We can find ourselves longing for God to answer our prayers and then discover that He provided exactly what we needed, even if it appeared to be different than what we asked for in prayer.

While writing this book and engaging in numerous conversations that provoke thoughts about understanding ***belonging***, God revealed something to me that I was able to share with a group of men, and now with you the reader. You previously read the story titled, "Rejection," which is located just a few stories earlier in this chapter. In that story you read about a man with a stutter who found acceptance, safety, and ***belonging*** in a Bible study group. His life has most likely been a constant search for those places for which he would be provided acceptance, safety, and ***belonging***. Once he found such a place, he desperately wanted to protect it. That place was a men's Bible study group called DIG (Digging into God). Since this group's existence, more than 15 years, very few men have decided to take part in the group.

Nearly all the men who have made the attempt to be part of the group have joined and remained. It is rare that a man will join us, and equally rare that he should leave us. The group is small, probably less than 25 total men. Each week there is an average of 15-18 who attend. Some of the men attend virtually, through video conferencing, and some of the men attend in person. Hardly a week goes by that someone in the group doesn't ask, "Why are men not joining our group?" This question has become both an anthem and a prayer for all the members.

While sitting with Dave, one of the men in the group, and discussing the elements of ***belonging***, Dave made a statement that brought a revelation to me. We were trying to understand why the group had remained relatively small, when Dave said, "DIG is the unknown group of our church." As soon as Dave declared this, God brought the revelation to me. God had protected us all these years so we could cultivate a culture of true *belonging*. It was an amazing and praiseworthy discovery. Dave needed me to clarify for him as he didn't quite understand his discovery.

I began asking Dave what was needed for *belonging* to exist. As we discussed this topic, many things were suggested. *Belonging* is much like the fruit of the Spirit; we can always have greater measures of it as there is an endless supply. It's similar to Psalm 34:8, every time you taste, it tastes better.

> *Psalm 34:8 (NIV), "Taste and see that the Lord is good; blessed is the one who takes refuge in him."*

We must know who we are, and Whose we are. Our identity is important. We must know that we have intrinsic value, and that the contribution of our gifts bring purpose. We must have a level of happiness that comes from knowing that someone is benefitting from our contribution, we are creating something together. We also must know that everyone is accepted into the group because tribalism breeds loyalty. If we are seeking truth, the gospel has no walls. All these elements must be present for *belonging* to exist.

So, God revealed to us that our group had been protected, all these years, so the culture of *belonging* could be manifested and acquired by all its members. What would happen if the group were to grow faster than the culture could be nurtured? The result would be that *belonging* would not be as prevalent, not entwined through all the members. It's likely that the newest members would experience something different than *belonging*. Perhaps they would find acceptance for themselves but would not want someone else to join the group and disrupt what they had found? Tribalism and loyalty might place a foothold in the door of the group. That is very possible, especially if they didn't have an identity grounded in Christ. The larger the group, the harder it is to find the *belonging* that people are searching for. What we have in this group is more precious than gold. God has blessed us, and we were finally ready to see it in a clearer way. We are His children, and we *belong* to Him.

Ephesians 1:3-5 (NIV), "Praise be to the God and Father of our Lord Jesus Christ, who has blessed us in the heavenly realms with every spiritual blessing in Christ. For he chose us in him before the creation of the world to be holy and blameless in his sight. In love he predestined us for adoption to sonship through Jesus Christ, in accordance with his pleasure and will."

Treasured

Romans 12:9 (NIV), "Love must be sincere. Hate what is evil; cling to what is good."

Sometimes we stumble onto things that we weren't seeking. When we finally see them, we're surprised that others are still blind to it. The innocence of those who are blind, coupled with the joy of those who really appreciate what they have is absolute bliss. A little more than a year after our son Michael died, our son Matthew was married to Rachael. My wife Laura and I desperately needed something to brighten up our days and Rachael was the joy that God prescribed. Since they have been married, we have gone on a couple of vacations together, enjoyed the holidays, and many family dinners. What makes this story so wonderful is that Rachael will often make this statement, "I am so blessed! I get to go on vacation with my whole family, I don't have to take two vacations. I get to be with everyone on the same vacation. I don't have to have two birthdays, two holidays, two dinners, or two of anything. I get to have *one* with everyone." Rachael can say that because Debbie and John, her mother and stepfather, are just as much an important and valued part of our family as my wife and I are. It's not something that we planned beforehand; it just sort of happened. When Rachael stated this the first time, I took notice of it. It brought a great sense of *belonging* to everyone.

This past Thanksgiving, we all sat around the kitchen table discussing what are we "thankful" for. Rachael started by saying, "I am thankful for carrying a healthy baby and looking forward to his arrival."

Matthew said, "I am thankful for my parents, my in-laws, as well as the coming arrival of our first child."

At this, my son David asked, "What is the big deal with the in-law thing? Why do you guys always make such a big deal about this?"

I said to David, "When it's my turn to share what I am thankful for, I will try and clear it up for you." After everyone else shared their thoughts on what they were thankful for, I stated, "I am thankful that my daughter Rachael can say that she doesn't have to take two vacations. She can be with her whole family on one vacation. I am also thankful that David will never understand the dilemma of the dreaded in-laws. He has never seen it, nor will he ever experience it, even after he marries Julia, our other ray of sunshine."

The same relationship my wife and I have with Rachael's parents is the same relationship we have with Julia's parents, Grace Ann and Mike. Sometimes ***belonging*** occurs when you don't see it coming. To me, it's the best when you don't have to try, it just happened. That's when you know the ***belonging*** you have should be treasured.

Praying

Ephesians 6:18 (NIV), "And pray in the Spirit on all occasions with all kinds of prayers and requests. With this in mind, be alert and always keep on praying for all the Lord's people."

I am privileged to be able to spend time with many groups of men in ministry and Bible study. The way that God weaves us together is nothing short of miraculous. It's rare that I find myself in a group where there isn't another man who shares multiple groups with me. For many years I have enjoyed a men's group on Saturday mornings at a local school. Even though I cannot always be present at their monthly meetings, I know that it is a group of men that I ***belong*** to. Within this group, I hear men speak of other groups that also meet on Saturday mornings, once a month. Rick is one of the men who has a group at his house. I have been invited to join his group multiple times, but it just never materialized. Several months ago, while Rick was talking, I sensed that he may be lonely. I was overwhelmed with compassion because Rick was hearing Satan tell him lies and he didn't know how to make it stop. That's when I told Rick, "I am going to make it a point to attend your group." Rick and I paired our calendars, so I knew the dates.

The first attempt at joining Rick's group failed. I thought I had entered the wrong date. However, Rick informed me that the previous month's meeting date had changed due to extenuating circumstances. When the next month arrived, I made sure to be in attendance. When I walked in, I knew a few of the men. As you might expect, I was greeted by everyone, was given coffee and some cookies. Then the leader of the group asked me to share a little about myself so everyone would know me better. Many questions were asked to clarify some of the brevity of my statements. It was then that something happened that changed everything. The leader handed out paper and pen to everyone and said that we were going to draw family trees of our immediate families. We would also include specific prayer requests for each of our family members. This diagram would provide a framework so every man in the group could be praying very specifically for all the other men's families. I was overcome with emotion. I have had many prayer interactions throughout my life. This is the first time this has ever happened to me. These men wanted to know who I was and what was important to me so they could be praying for my family and me. Many of the men were just meeting me for the first time and this is the welcome that I received. I looked at Rick and couldn't thank him enough for extending the invitation to be a part of his group. I knew in that moment that I *belonged* with these men. I knew that God always knows best. Not all the men who *belong* to that group were present that day, but thank you Rick, Doug, Eddie, Scott, Dick, and Todd for making me feel that I *belong*.

-Lessons Learned-

We all want *belonging*. God deposited this desire in each of us. The world we live in can sometimes make this desire challenging to fulfill. I desperately hope that you find Jesus on your journey, the source and power of all our *belonging*, as only He can truly satisfy that need. With our identity firmly rooted in Him, our *belonging* will continually flourish.

You belong to the God who created the universe…and He is able to do far more than you could ever ask, think, or imagine. (Author Unknown)

2

Blinded by Loyalty

There are many places we search and hope for ***belonging***, unfortunately most of them leave us wanting to ***belong*** even more. If Christ is not at the center of our ***belonging***, there will always be something missing, a significant lacking. That's because we are His creation, and we ***belong*** to Him. Our families are supposed to provide, in fact they are designed to provide, our preliminary degree of understanding for our ***belonging***. As we grow up and become more social, we will find ourselves leaning on our friends for ***belonging***. Because we crave ***belonging***, we are almost always willing to change our identity for ***belonging***. This is when we identify as our vocation, political stance, worldview, our crisis, or even our circumstances. Searching and finding our identity horizontally will always lead to comparison and the need for approval. Comparison never fulfills or sustains. Man's approval will always require renewal. We look for the approval of others and where we can fit-in, even if we don't agree with their concepts. Groups of various kinds help us to temporarily ease the ache for ***belonging***. Sports teams, political parties, workplace assemblies, church ministries, clubs, and even gangs are just a few of the groups where we search for ***belonging***. We utilize all these different clusters of people to give us what we desire. However, once again if Christ is not at the center, there will always be a lack.

If our identity is not found in Christ, because we have allowed it to be determined by the world, the pursuit of truth normally takes a backseat, and loyalty takes its place. Think of your identity in this way. Suppose your car was about to careen into a body of water. There would be an emotional explosion erupting inside of you followed by a desperate attempt to escape the car for fear you may drown. Whenever your identity is not found in Christ, this same type of explosion erupts inside of you when you hear something that is different from what you have attached your identity to.

Anything that differs from your devoted attachment, causes such a person to fight as if their very existence depended on it, much like drowning in a body of water. For any of us to find **belonging**, we must be rooted in Christ, the only unifier, else we continue to draw lines of division. Otherwise, **belonging** will continue to elude us.

If we hang out with or spend our time with people who are *only* loyal, we will find ourselves surrounded by what I refer to as "yes" men. In my first book, "How Do I Love My Neighbor," I highlight that I will never be your "yes" man. "Yes" men do not share the truth. In fact, a group of yes men will eventually become a tribe. Loyalty often does not breed growth or sharing, especially when loyalty is not accompanied by truth. Tribalism forms when loyalty is the aim. In most cases, even those where Christ is meant to be present, there is a danger for tribalism (a strong loyalty to a party or group) to occur. Striving for **belonging** can create separation and division, instead of unity. Often, when a person hungers and pangs through a long season to find **belonging** and believes they have found such a place, a form of narcissism can set in. "It's mine" is the basis that it's all about *me*. Any thought of including others causes an offense. A person gets offended when their ungodly desires are being exploited or examined by someone asking questions directed at the truth.

Groups with strong religious convictions and staunch political beliefs are some of the most unattractive, yet loyal, tribal groups that create the greatest divisions of all. What's more, many of the people in these groups claim Christian virtue while desecrating anyone who differs from their view. Their anthem very closely resembles this, "If you don't believe and behave exactly as I do, you can't **belong**." Sometimes this anthem is internally silent, but most often the anthem is loudly, and proudly spoken. It would appear that there is no end to the amount of evil that man could accomplish if he could be unified apart from God. Perhaps that is why God scattered all the people at the Tower of Babel.

Genesis 11:4-6 (NIV), 'Then they said, "Come, let us build ourselves a city, with a tower that reaches to the heavens, so that we may make a name for ourselves; otherwise, we will be scattered over the face of the whole earth." But the Lord came down to see the city and the tower the people were building. The Lord said, "If as one people speaking the same language they have begun to do this, then nothing they plan to do will be impossible for them." '

Fear is the cause of much of the tribalism among certain groups. Two such groups include gangs and political parties. Both groups incite fear in their members. If a person is not loyal to the cause, fear of what will happen takes over. Many a person is caught behind enemy lines and stays in the group out of fear. A person may perform many tasks for the group that don't necessarily benefit them, nor are they generally creative, but they perform them anyway out of fear. If you want to leave the gang, it may cost you your life. If you don't think, talk, and act just as the political group warrants, you will be thrown out. One group won't let you leave alive, the other group will throw you away. Loyalty as the primary focus is never good, but if it is secondary or supplements seeking truth, unity can prevail. It's important to understand what **belonging** is not. **Belonging** is not tribalism. All the people who greeted Jesus on His triumphant march into Jerusalem had something in common. All hailed to the One that is our Savior, Hosanna, and it united them all. He was acknowledged as the source.

Matthew 21:9 (NIV), 'The crowds that went ahead of him and those that followed shouted, "Hosanna to the Son of David!" "Blessed is he who comes in the name of the Lord!" "Hosanna in the highest heaven!" '

When shouts of "Hosanna" turned into threats of "crucify Him," tribalism won out. Tribes are based on desire, or fear of the future, or receiving loyalty from each other. In tribalism, a person or group gains something from someone but it is not a shared experience. Tribalism is dividing. **Belonging** is uniting. Peter had to be corrected by Paul because he was wrong. Peter's loyalty in Galatians, Chapter 2, was his highest priority. As often happens, it leads to ruin.

*Galatians 2:11-21 (NIV), 'When Cephas came to Antioch, I opposed him to his face, because he stood condemned. For before certain men came from James, he used to eat with the Gentiles. But when they arrived, he began to draw back and separate himself from the Gentiles because he was afraid of those who **belonged** to the circumcision* *group. The other Jews joined him in his hypocrisy, so that by their hypocrisy even Barnabas was led astray. When I saw that they were not acting in line with the truth of the gospel, I said to Cephas in front of them all, "You are a Jew, yet you live like a Gentile and not like a Jew. How is it, then, that you force Gentiles to follow Jewish customs? "We who are Jews by birth and not sinful Gentiles know that a person is not justified by the works of the law, but by faith in Jesus Christ. So we, too, have put our faith in Christ Jesus that we may be justified by faith in Christ and not by the works of the law, because by the works of the law no one will be justified. "But if, in seeking to be justified in Christ, we Jews find ourselves also among the sinners, doesn't that mean that Christ promotes sin? Absolutely not! If I rebuild what I destroyed, then I really would be a lawbreaker. "For through the law I died to the law so that I might live for God. I have been crucified with Christ and I no longer live, but Christ lives in me. The life I now live in the body, I live by faith in the Son of God, who loved me and gave himself for me. I do not set aside the grace of God, for if righteousness could be gained through the law, Christ died for nothing!"*

Most everyone knows a person or two who can be very aggressive in terms of politics or religion. Whenever there is strife in these areas, one can be sure that the person causing division has determined that theirs *is* the only way. They have already decided, there is *no* other way. They won't hear you unless you line up with their way of thinking. It is quite interesting when you think about it. Which one of us would walk into a room of 50 people and boldly declare, "My vantage point is the only one that matters? Everyone else's view is worth spit." Assuming that there are infinite vantage points in a room, or any situation, why would a person who claims to know more or better make such a foolhardy boast? The answer is simple, their identity is found in something of the world, it is not found in Christ. When your identity is not found in Christ, but found in something other, division will always remain. Loyalty remains primary, conflict evident, and ***belonging*** obscure. With wrong identity, and ***belonging*** absent, peacemaking is never possible.

James 3:17 (NIV), "But the wisdom that comes from heaven is first of all pure; then peace-loving, considerate, submissive, full of mercy and good fruit, impartial and sincere."

Wedding

Romans 16:17 (NIV) "I urge you, brothers and sisters, to watch out for those who cause divisions and put obstacles in your way that are contrary to the teaching you have learned. Keep away from them."

At the church where I worship, I have the pleasure of leading a Pastoral Care Ministry with a small group of co-leaders. This ministry is very intense in terms of training. Each of the participants must immerse themselves through 20 weeks of skill modules designed to prepare them to walk with people who are experiencing seasons of grief, trials, tribulations, or suffering. Because of the length of the training, we only provide it once a year. Often, we are contacted by smaller churches, in the surrounding area, to determine if we would be willing to include them in our training. Of course, we run an open-door policy which means we will train anyone who would like to join us, even if they do not attend our church, or are part of a different denomination. Sometimes those individuals will remain in our ministry as their church may be too small to accommodate one or they may not have an active ministry. Additionally, every training is coordinated with another (partner) church. This provides the trainees with the option to attend a module on a different day in the event that an emergency should arise. The partner church adjusts their schedule to a different day and usually a week or two behind.

Cheryl was a person looking to train with us and she was from a different church, one that did not have an active Pastoral Care Ministry. When Cheryl arrived at our building on the first day of training, she examined the schedule which listed the (partner) church. Cheryl discovered that the (partner) church was within a mile from her home.

At the end of the first training, Cheryl approached me and said, "Jeff, seeing that the partner church is less than a mile from my house, perhaps it would be better for me to take the training there instead of here."

I replied, "Cheryl, if that would make your life easier, then by all means, please attend the training at the alternate church." After the following week of training, I received a phone call from Cheryl.

She stated, "I think I made a mistake and want to know if you could help."

So, I asked Cheryl, "How can I help? What seems to be the matter?"

Cheryl replied, "When I attended the training, everything seemed to be going really well. But at the end, the instructor approached me and said that because I was not one of *their* members, I was free to attend their training, but there was no way I would be permitted to minister as part of their ministry. Basically, I don't **belong** because I am not one of *them*."

I immediately told Cheryl that she made no mistake, and if she was willing, she could come back to our training. Cheryl was so excited and relieved. When the training was complete, Cheryl joined us in our active ministry where she ministered to many people. She was a part of the peer group that I facilitated, and she remained with us for a few years. One day, a year or so, after Cheryl had left the ministry, she contacted me. She was looking for someone to preside over her daughter's marriage ceremony. She asked if I was willing to be that person. Without hesitation, I agreed. The wedding was held at a beautiful site, a few hours' drive for everyone. The day was spectacular. The bride and groom were joyous, and I got to meet many from Cheryl's family. As I was driving home, I pondered how it came to be that I would be part of this event. The simple answer is this, **belonging** won over tribalism. However, there was more. Sometimes we search for **belonging** in earnest, and sometimes we find it when we aren't looking. In Cheryl's case, she found **belonging**, but comfort and ease were more important. However, when tribalism removed her peace, she returned to the place she knew she **belonged**.

Unthinkable

1 Timothy 4:1-3 (NIV), "The Spirit clearly says that in later times some will abandon the faith and follow deceiving spirits and things taught by demons. Such teachings come through hypocritical liars, whose consciences have been seared as with a hot iron. They forbid people to marry and order them to abstain from certain foods, which God created to be received with thanksgiving by those who believe and who know the truth."

I am very blessed in the fact that I have the privilege of spending lots of time with a lot of different people because of the nature of my ministry. Sometimes a long-term relationship develops and other times we share only one or two meetings together. I have a friend, Mike, who I have known for more than 20 years. Mike and I have shared many ministry moments together over the years and I always attempt to help him along his faith journey. There came a day when Mike asked me to visit his new church. He was very excited and wanted me to meet his new pastor. Although it took a bit of creative scheduling, we were finally able to select a Sunday to be together and partake in the service at his church. When we arrived, I was surprised by the number of people that I knew from previous Bible studies, different churches, and ministries. I introduced Mike to each of the people I knew and then spent a couple of minutes getting reacquainted. The service was delightful, and Mike's pastor displayed a great command of the Scriptures.

After the service was over, some of the people that I knew gathered around and we talked at greater length. One of the persons who approached me was a woman that I knew from a previous church. She, and her family, were both very surprised but also very pleased that I had attended the church service. She asked if I was going to become a member. I let her know that I was just visiting at the request of my friend Mike. She then redirected our conversation toward her new understanding of the gospel. While attending this church she believed she heard the gospel for the first time in her life, because of the way the pastor shared the Word of God. She said she had been a Christian her whole life, but at the age of 52 she finally understood the gospel.

At this she started to tell me all the people she had walked away from. She mentioned both friends and family members that she could no longer, nor wanted to, spend time with because they were heathens, sinners, and wretched.

I had to ask, "Are you sure it was the gospel you heard?"

She said, "I never received the gospel in my life. Not from my family church, while growing up, and not from the previous church where you and I once worshiped together. But here, in this church, I have been filled with the Holy Spirit."

I said to her, "I think it's fantastic that you are filled with the Holy Spirit. But why are you removing people from your life?"

She stated, "How can I continue to spend time with these people, they are worldly sinners who dance at weddings and use words that I can't repeat."

To which I asked, "Weren't you once a worldly sinner? Are you now looking down on people? Aren't you a sinner saved by grace? Don't you want everyone to have what you have received?"

Again, she asked, "How can I spend time with people who actively sin?"

At this, I asked her, "Where did Jesus spend His time?"

She replied, "I know He spent time with sinners."

I stated, "If you know that, and He is the One we follow and emulate, where do you think you should spend your time? Aren't you supposed to be a light in the dark?" I could tell she was now becoming very frustrated.

Then she asked, "Why are you still attending that church? I never received the gospel from that church. If a church doesn't share the gospel, then it's not a church it is in fact a cult."

To this I asked, "Why are you not only judging the body of Christ, but actively speaking negatively against it? Churches should not speak negatively against other churches, and Christians should not speak negatively against other Christians. In fact, Christians should not speak negatively against anyone. Unity is only possible through Jesus Christ. Whosoever *will* is the gospel invitation. This is the only principle of inclusion or exclusion. A spirit that is not large enough to embrace all the children of God has been poisoned already."

At this she said, "I have never been able to read the Word. I know that you read it, and it is apparent that you know it, but I have never been able to read it. I love listening to this pastor, he shares like no one I have ever heard."

At this, I warned, "If you are not in the Word, you are missing out on the revelation of God. The one place where He speaks to us the most, you have forsaken. Please remember, the pastor's job is not to feed you. His job is to make you hungry. Church is not supposed to be your filling station. You are to be filled all week long and then come together as one body of believers to worship." She continued to disagree. And then things went from bad to worse.

As we were talking, another woman approached us. She introduced herself as Linda and then asked my name. She then asked, "Is this your first time at this church?"

To which I said, "Yes it is."

She turned to my friend and said, "I have seen you here before. How long have you been attending?" My friend stated she and her family had been attending for almost a year. Then Linda looked back at me and said, "I just wanted you to know that each of these seats have invisible names on them."

I interrupted her and asked, "Did I sit in your seat?"

Linda stated, "Yes you did. I want you to know that I was quite perturbed to find you sitting in my seat. I even told my friend Bonnie that my seat was being occupied by someone other than me. I want you to know, it took a lot of self-control to not bring this to your attention before the service began. But Jeff, I held back. So, Jeff, I am telling you that it was fine that you sat in my seat today, but come next week, you better not be in my seat."

I replied, "No worries Linda, I assure you that I will not be in your seat next week."

Then she laughed and said, "Goodbye." I ended my conversation with my friend and headed back home.

We should never mistake the bad behavior of some people as the representation of the whole. However, I did not experience a sense of *belonging*. More than anything else, there was a dividing and not a unifying culture. This is further proof that even in the church, *belonging* is not always imparted to you. What would have happened if I was brand new to the Christian faith and happened to walk into this church looking for *belonging*? More than likely, I would have done what many have done, for generations, when they experience such hypocrisy from the church. I probably would have run as far away from the church as possible. Maybe never to return. Again, it must be said that we should never use the behavior of a single person or even a couple of people to provide our sense of *belonging*.

Hopefully, you will never experience what happened to me when you enter a new church. One woman claimed to find what she had been looking for her whole life, the gospel. After finding it, she decided to keep it for herself as it wasn't worth sharing. Ironically, we are to share the gospel with everyone as it is the good news. A different woman wanted what she felt was hers, her seat. She begrudgingly shared it once because she had to. She arrived late for the service and feared she might look unrighteous before the congregation if she said anything. However, she warned me afterwards that she would never share it again. I was sternly warned privately, I had better not dare sit in her chair again. Neither of these ladies had received **belonging**, so it wasn't something they could share.

Poached

Proverbs 25:26 (NIV), "Like a muddied spring or a polluted well are the righteous who give way to the wicked."

After I wrote my first book, I decided that I would reach out to the local bookstores to determine if there was any interest in having a book signing. Many of the bookstores in my area participated by allowing me to spend an afternoon in their store believing it would draw more customers as well as helping me to gain exposure. Unfortunately, most of the larger bookstore chains were not interested. When I had finally exhausted all the stores who would be willing to cooperate, I decided that I would attempt to share my book with the local churches in my area. I have a friend, Dave, who had invited me to a couple of his church's men's gatherings. Both Dave and I believed that this was the most likely place to begin. I reached out to the ministry leaders, via email, to see if they would be interested in having a cup of coffee to discuss the idea. Since Dave had already introduced us, both men appeared very excited about the possibility. However, we had an extremely difficult time trying to find a day and time to meet. After some persistence, we finally sat down for coffee.

We spoke about the need for men to become spiritually mature. We shared some of our stories of how God had strengthened our faith and brought us to understand our leadership abilities and the roles we were in. We spoke at length about our growing congregations and the need to break down walls. We inspired each other concerning the gospel. Each of us shared our belief that the gospel is indeed the "Good News" and brings unity. We commented that if it were to bring division, it is not understood by the person sharing it. The thought of sharing with other men about my book, "How Do I Love My Neighbor," appealed to them. They stated that each of us can always get better at loving our neighbor. The meeting lasted almost two hours.

Then one of the leaders stated, "Please understand, anything new brought into our church would first need to be run by our lead pastor. He would be the one to say (yes) or (no)."

I replied, "I have no problem waiting for the approval of your lead pastor and will respect his decision." Our meeting appeared to be winding down, so we began sharing our thanks for coming and looking forward to meeting again soon.

It was then that one of the men leaned over and asked one final question, "You're not planning on poaching some of our men, are you?"

Hearing his question, I was quite stunned. I didn't want to react in a way that was aggressive. So, I held my emotions in check and said, "I have no plans of poaching anyone. And I am not sure why you would ask me that question."

He exclaimed, "We need to make sure that our congregation is protected. You can never be too sure."

I replied, "I can assure you that I am in no way planning to do anything that even remotely resembles poaching anyone. I have been to a couple of your men's meetings and have even been introduced to some of your men. I simply thought that this was an opportunity for us to work together. Please forgive me if I have somehow led you to believe that it was ever my intention to poach your men."

When I left the meeting, I started thinking about some of the things we had talked about. It was clear to me that I did not **belong** in their church. It was also clear to me that my time spent with them would not bear any fruit. I pray for those in leadership who believe their congregation **belongs** to them. I pray they one day realize that we are all on the same team, and the body of Christ, every church, **belongs** to God.

Misplaced

2 Corinthians 6:14 (NIV), "Do not be yoked together with unbelievers. For what do righteousness and wickedness have in common? Or what fellowship can light have with darkness?"

Long before I became a follower of Jesus Christ, there were many instances in my life where I chose loyalty over truth. I did this because I had no concept of the difference as there was no one in my life to direct me in that way. As I have indicated previously, loyalty is a great quality, but it must be a supporting quality, not standing on its own. Loyalty must be in addition to something such as searching for truth. If loyalty stands on its own, we will make choices that help us remain in our comfort, division will continue, unity will always be concealed, and we will never grow in maturity. Here is a story of two men, one who was loyal, and one who was a seeker of truth.

One day, I walked into the fabrication shop where I was employed. Most people did not like entering this place because Scott, the manager, was the crudest, rudest, and nastiest person I have ever met in my life. That day, I walked into the fabrication shop to find Rob pinned in the corner by Scott. Scott was calling Rob all sorts of foul things. He was pushing, punching, and belittling Rob! Why? Why would someone do such a thing? As Rob walked into the fab shop that day, Scott was gazing at a porno magazine and wanted Rob to look as well. Rob refused! Why? Rob was a Christian! But the more Rob refused, the angrier Scott became and the more he physically accosted Rob. As I watched this unfold in front of me, I began to cheer Scott on. Yes, you heard me correctly. It pains me to share this story. I was both *in* the world and *of* the world at that time.

James 4:4 (NIV), "You adulterous people, don't you know that friendship with the world means enmity against God? Therefore, anyone who chooses to be a friend of the world becomes an enemy of God."

I was not a Christian at that time, but I was a human being that could have responded differently. Still, I did nothing to stop this from happening. Why did I do nothing? I did nothing because I was loyal to the group that I was a part of. I did nothing because I was fearful of not being a part of my group. I didn't care about truth, I only cared about myself. Remember, self-preservation always places the relationship at a far distant second. If I had done anything different, I would live in fear, running the risk of being rejected. You could say that I would lose my *belonging* to the worldly people if I had any courage to stand up for truth. However, I didn't even know what *belonging* meant at that time. I only cared that I was loyal to my group.

What occurred thereafter, astounded me. This godly man, Rob, watched me watch him be physically and verbally assaulted for not wanting to dishonor his God. He watched me cheer this event on and still Rob decided that I was worth loving. Rob had every reason to never speak to me, to never forgive me, even to hate me. However, to my surprise, that day Rob decided to make me his friend. Rob *belonged* to the kingdom of God, and he wanted to show me that I could *belong* as well. That day, I watched someone stand up for something bigger than himself. I was not sure what that something was, all I knew was that Rob was willing to be persecuted for it. He became the first person to not only speak truth to me, but to show me that truth is worth fighting for. Rob shared many things with me and helped me begin a journey, the best journey I have ever known! Where did Rob come from? I did not search him out. God brought us together.

God's grace is enough! It is this grace that brings forth change. Seekers of truth bring about change because seekers of truth work to remove division. Those who have true *belonging* are those who can give *belonging*. Many of us settle for a cheap imitation, something that we have justified in our minds. I pray that one day you are greatly interrupted by truth. I pray it awakens you to confront your own false beliefs. On the other side of that struggle, you are sure to find *belonging*.

> *John 17:20-23 (NIV), "My prayer is not for them alone. I pray also for those who will believe in me through their message, that all of them may be one, Father, just as you are in me and I am in you. May they also be in us so that the world may believe that you have sent me. I have given them the glory that you gave me, that they may be one as we are one— I in them and you in me—so that they may be brought to complete unity. Then the world will know that you sent me and have loved them even as you have loved me."*

Division

1 Corinthians 1:10 (NIV), "I appeal to you, brothers and sisters, in the name of our Lord Jesus Christ, that all of you agree with one another in what you say and that there be no divisions among you, but that you be perfectly united in mind and thought."

I have had the pleasure of experiencing many mission trips. Most of these trips have been enjoyed in the company of my friends. The first trip we embarked on together took us to Connecticut. On this trip, however, I only knew one person, the friend who invited me. Of course, I would get to know many more along the way as traveling from Michigan to Connecticut would provide many opportunities to share. Piling 44 people in three 15-passenger vans made our ride very close for comfort and very exhausting. As we set out, I was unsure of what to expect along the way or what was awaiting us when we arrived.

I recall feeling slightly unsettled before we departed for Connecticut because I was the only person who didn't **belong** to the denominational church from which we set out from. I **belonged** to a different church. Everyone was kind and pleasant and made me feel welcomed. The conversation in the vehicles was plentiful for a couple of reasons. First, this was going to be a very long ride. Second, there were 43 other people that I could have a conversation with. Lastly, it was customary for this group to perform a mass-distribution drill where every person was required to switch vehicles and seats whenever we made a stop for gas, bathroom, dining, or hotel, etc. This allowed every person the opportunity to get to know everyone on the trip.

On the second day of travel to Connecticut, I remember a conversation with one of the women in the group. She asked me what church I attended. I told her that I attended a non-denominational church. Her reply was a bit startling. She said, "That sounds like watered down religion to me." I know she wasn't attempting to be combative or even disrespectful, but her comment was clothed in loyalty. She drew an invisible circle around herself, and I was not allowed to enter. She made it clear that I was not one of them. Suddenly my **belonging** was stripped from me even though I was supposed to be part of the group.

My reply to her caused her to pause as she was stunned. I said, "Call it whatever you like, but somehow 15,000 people are walking through the doors every Sunday." When we arrived at our destination, I was given a tour and provided the lowdown of the daily operations for the week. Some 300-400 people had traveled from across the country, from more than 50 churches and multiple religious denominations for the purpose of converging on a community for one week to provide house repairs of various kinds. It was my first experience of this kind.

The rules were simple. The entire group of people would be broken down into many smaller groups made up of two adults and five teenage children. The twist here is that you would not be in a group with anyone that you traveled with. You would be placed in a group made up of people that you did not know and spend the entire week working together as a team while learning about each other. Upon returning each night back to the school where everyone was lodging, you would then return to the group from whom you traveled with and have a Bible study and some fellowship. During the second night of our fellowship, I was asked a question and I shared my thoughts. This led me to share even more throughout the night. As we began to retire for the night, the woman who said, "That sounds like watered down religion," approached me. She asked, "How is it that you can talk about God like that? How do you share so passionately and freely?"

I responded, "YOU said that I had watered down religion. I want you to know that I don't have a religion. I have a relationship with the God of the Universe. He knows my name. I know Him and I am known by Him."

To this she asked, "But how do you speak like that?"

I exclaimed, "Are you thankful and grateful for the gift of grace and mercy that God lavishes on you each day?"

She said, "Yes, of course!"

I replied, "Then tell everyone. In the same way that you would rave over a great meal at a restaurant, or a powerful movie you watched at the theater, share what God has done in your life whenever you can. When you do it, do it with gladness and excitement. The God of all creation has set you free of sin, guilt, and shame. He has provided a way when there was no way. You get to live with Him in paradise. Share all the wonderful things that God has done!" As she walked away, she appeared to be in deep thought.

This mission trip and the many others I have taken like it have caused me to sit in deep thought at times, just like the watered-down religion woman. How can Christians come together in large groups and sometimes feel unified and other times feel separated, as if they do not ***belong***? The trip to Connecticut had more than 50 churches made up of more than 12 denominations united for a common purpose. If the purpose for which we united remained the focus, unity was in place. Each person could leverage their gifting toward helping someone, knowing that they had intrinsic value and had contributed uniquely to something bigger. However, it appeared that as soon as we lost focus of why we gathered, unity would escape us. Loyalty would set in, and everyone would return to their respective denominations. Is this the way Christianity should be lived out? Furthermore, if we, Christians, break down into smaller factions, our denominations, are we allowing loyalty to become an idol over unity in the body of Christ? Truth in Christianity is unity and ***belonging***.

> *Ephesians 4:1-6 (NIV), "As a prisoner or the Lord, then, I urge you to live a life worthy of the calling you have received. Be completely humble and gentle; be patient, bearing with one another in love. Make every effort to keep the unity of the Spirit through the bond of peace. There is one body and one Spirit, just as you were called to one hope when you were called; one Lord, one faith, one baptism; one God and Father of all, who is over all and through all and in all."*

-Lessons Learned-

We all have blind spots, some have more than others. The weird thing about being blind is you can't see. The truth is right in front of you, but you are unable to do anything about it. People who are spiritually blind don't know they are blind. Many groups offer loyalty, but with that loyalty often comes fear. If there is fear attached to your group, ***belonging*** will never materialize. It's easy to misplace your identity in something that we believe provides purpose. If you want to find purpose, don't go looking for your purpose, look for the Purpose Giver. When you find your Creator, you find you. Only in this way will ***belonging*** both fulfill and sustain.

Identity Matters

I allow My sheep to be gathered under shepherds I have called to share in My work. The hearts of these leaders belong to Me. They hear my voice clearly and lead My sheep in truth and love. (Author Unknown)

3

Implements, Ill-Designed for the Purpose

Psalm 42:3 (NIV), 'My tears have been my food day and night, while people say to me all day long, "Where is your God?"'

The day I found out my son Michael had died from a Fentanyl overdose, there was an immediate and continued rush of confusion. My mind could not and would not function properly. I was frantically trying to get home to my wife, my thoughts racing, not believing what I had just heard. In some ways, there still exists a "consciousness of famine" that may well saddle me all my days. When people say shock brings with it the absence of reality, the inability to think, to see, to hear, or to understand plainly, when you are close-up to the death of someone you loved, one begins to comprehend what that might mean. Each person experiences the highs and lows of life differently. Each of our experiences are filtered through both a private and a public sentience. What is going on in our minds, during traumatic moments, may appear to the world vastly different from what we are displaying. Even in cases of extreme emotional distress, what seems to be a likely conclusion can never be fully accounted for by the observer. That day has forever changed my family, my marriage, my relationship with God, and my view of the world.

Each day that passed while my family and I waited for the coming of Michael's funeral, brought with it the influx of further emotions. Tears began to fall without warning, and they would not stop. I found myself falling asleep crying. I was waking up crying. I was crying uncontrollably throughout each new day. I was crying from pain, exhaustion, emotional stress, deep loss, and want. I cried, until it became apparent that tears would be my food for many days, and then I cried some more. It was relentless, never stopping, the pain was excruciating. I began to long and search with directed hope that through my tears, maybe, perhaps, I shall see things that dry-eyed I could not. Other than longing for Michael's return, desperately wanting him back, I could only ponder, what do I do with these salt-drenched eyes. I prayed, "Oh God, please help me make sense of my new life."

When the day of Michael's funeral arrived, there was an unexpected silence in my life. It was quiet like never before. Very few words were spoken between me and my wife. I don't remember speaking to my sons or daughters. But we had to get ready to view Michael for the first time since the police officer showed us his picture at the scene. We were also getting ready to say goodbye because we would never see him again. It's the never ending "barrenness" that is so painful! It won't stop! There's nothing I can do to make it stop! Nothing prepares you for such an experience. Walking in and seeing Michael laying in the casket, I don't know? There are still no words. The pain of suffering is a guest to many. One day, the guest became a permanent resident. I remember when joy was still my lot. Now it's different. We have been graced with the strength to endure, but we have been assaulted!

During the fellowship time of Michael's funeral viewing, there were two distinct moments that made it clear I now **belonged** to a new club. This club is one that no one willingly joins, a club you avoid at all costs, a club from which I can never escape. First, I randomly received a text message from a person I had yet to meet. This person said something that I have never forgotten. His message read, "I have a license to talk to you. Today, I will begin praying for you. When you are ready, I will be here." With this message, it appeared that the club members almost came looking for me. Of course, they simply wanted me to know they were here for me. Still, it was apparent that I now had a "license" as well.

Next, there was a strange exchange between some of the people I was greeting upon entry into the funeral home. Some of the people who offered their condolences actually needed me to minister to them. It was the strangest thing. I was angry the first time it happened. I remember asking God, "Really? This is what you want? Today, of all days?.... Okay God. I'll do it." When this grossly irregular shift happened four or five more times, I began to laugh inside. I thought, "This cannot be happening."

That is when God spoke to me, as clearly as I have ever heard Him before. He said, "Do you think I don't know what this feels like? I am right here. I have not left you. We will get through this. We will get through this together." I don't know why, but those words brought an instant identity of being God's child and **belonging** to something more powerful than I could comprehend. I was unaware at that time, but the words God shared with me that day were not just for that day. God meant it for the rest of my days, but I could not see it clearly at that moment.

The pain of losing a child? How can anyone begin to adequately describe it? I asked my friend, and artist, Steve Perucca to sketch his rendering of two statues that exist for public view. Both are someone's interpretation of what it means to experience the grief of losing a loved one. The first statue is called "Emptiness," by artist Albert Gyorgy, located in Switzerland. This is a statue of a figure sitting down, slouching with its head bowed and its arms crossed with forearms resting on its thighs. One can tell by the posture that the image is expressing sorrow. The whole chest cavity is missing, its breath is gone because it has lost a child. Part of the figure is missing. Part of *me* has been missing since 7/7/2019.

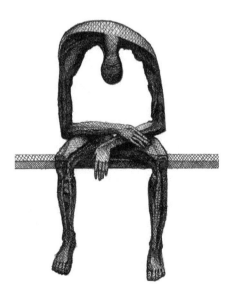

(Sketch by Steve Perucca)

The second statue is called "The Weight of Grief," by artist Celeste Roberge, located in Reno, Nevada. This is a statue of a steel rebar basket-woven figure crouched in the fetal position. The figure is filled with rocks. One can tell by the posture that the image is expressing pain: the deep agonizing pain of grief.

(Sketch by Steve Perucca)

I have often shared these two sketches in an attempt to describe how it feels to lose a child. If you were to combine the sketches, it might make better sense. However, there is more. Imagine combining the imagery of both the sketches while in a place of total darkness and you are groping along like a blind person with great uncertainty, searching and feeling about with pronounced angst. The pain of losing a child constantly gropes about your soul, frantically looking for a place to land. The pain never stops reminding you. Never! But then you encounter another parent, one who has tasted this unrelenting agony. God does something amazing amid the hurt, the sorrow, and the suffering. God brings peace, even if it's only temporary. And you then realize, there is a **belonging** and a comfort that you never expected to find in the direst of circumstances. It's like an extra inheritance, a blessing, even from the one we have lost, going to someone who needs what we have to give. *So, we are refreshed by the memory of the loved one, and at the same time we are offering a gift.*

2 Corinthians 1:3-4 (NIV), "Praise be to the God and Father of our Lord Jesus Christ, the Father of compassion and the God of all comfort, who comforts us in all our troubles, so that we can comfort those in any trouble with the comfort we ourselves receive from God."

Sharing

Colossians 1:20 (NIV), "and through him to reconcile to himself all things, whether things on earth or things in heaven, by making peace through his blood, shed on the cross."

The cross is a graphic demonstration of the depth of God's love. The willing and humble act of the radical obedience of Christ to the Father on behalf of humanity provides a sober observation of the seriousness of sin and the fallen human condition. Is this the divine solution to the human predicament that God would turn an instrument of execution into an *implement* of peace? The mystery of God is often confounding. I have learned that common sense will never get us closer to Jesus. I have also learned that God takes the most traumatic events of our lives and uses them as implements, ill-designed for the purpose, to bring restoration and healing.

I would eventually meet Hank, that man who texted me on the day of Michael's funeral. Remember, his message said, "I have a license to talk to you. Today I will begin praying for you. When you are ready, I will be here." Hank lived up to his words, as he and I spent a few meetings together, drawing from each other's strength. The **belonging** we had, we never wanted, but we could not have been closer as we shed our tears in the presence of someone who had walked a mile in our shoes. The grief we both felt, the pain we shared, the numbing of our countenance was somehow softened when we were together. I don't know how to explain it, but the **belonging** we both abhorred was also an *implement* of healing. It's a costly wisdom, losing a child, and God knows we did not ask for it. But it is also true that our coming through a great sorrow can make us stronger and remind us of what is truly important.

My son Michael was the fourth son in three generations of my family to leave us too soon. My dad's brother Larry died at the age of 31. My cousin Greg died at the age of 25. My cousin Jason died at the age of 41. Although these deaths affected me as they would anyone else, I did not truly internalize them or give them the proper attention until Michael. He was just 22. In addition to my family members, I had known other friends, and friends of friends, who had also experienced this awful tragedy. But Hank was the first person I encountered with a new consciousness of *belonging*, because now it was like a coat that I would never take off again.

In the three years since Michael's death, God has brought many people with this same affliction into my company, 52 in total to date. I never asked for any of them, nor did I search for them, I didn't even see them until God's timing was made perfect. The words that God shared with me, *"Do you think I don't know how this feels? We will get through this. We will get through this together,"* produced greater clarity as time went on. Of the 52 appointments, two parents lost their only child, four parents lost two children (one lost two in the same moment), and one parent lost three children. In the way that only God can, His divine intervention would alter our state of being as our paths crossed, when our *belonging* was made apparent.

"For we have shared many griefs, but they are translated into pure love and rejoicing when we meet. What makes our hearts rise with joy when we meet again people with whom we have shared a sorrow? We have all heard of the guilt of the survivor--the person who wonders why he or she has been spared when someone else has perished. Perhaps there's such a thing, after some time for healing has passed, as the joy of the survivor—not in any gloating or triumphant way, but in simple acknowledgement that, having come through severe testing and anguish, one is alive and has been able to modulate that grief into a life that is productive and to a large degree joyful. We have passed through fire and not been destroyed. We have, in fact, been reborn. Because when our loved one died, something in us died, too—some expectation or hope of a future together. And out of the ashes of that destroyed dream we have been lifted to new life. And when we find someone for whom this is also

true—especially if that is someone with whom we have shared grief in the past—why, of course we are filled with love and rejoicing! What else?

In the fellowship of those reborn out of grief we are all brothers and sisters. There, we find belonging!" (Martha Hickman, "Healing After Loss")

Ordainment

Psalm 23:6 (NIV), "Surely your goodness and love will follow me all the days of my life, and I will dwell in the house of the Lord forever."

One Sunday morning I was invited by two of my mentors and friends, Loren Siffring and Ron Daggett, to witness an ordination they would be performing. We were to travel about three and one-half hours away to accommodate this special occasion. When we arrived, there were approximately 100 people who were in attendance to support the man who was to be ordained, of which I was barely acquainted. Not knowing anyone else, I mingled within the crowd and then settled in with a man who appeared to be both welcoming and talkative. When we had spent nearly an hour in fellowship the ordainment was to begin. I sat next to the man who I had just met. Ordainment is not the beginning of something, it is the acknowledgement of what is already present. When there is evidence that a person is living for the purpose of sharing the gospel of Jesus, and there is a fruit bearing ministry, that person can be ordained. This is in no way a license that someone studies to achieve, it is a lifestyle to live.

After the prearranged guidelines for the ordination were fulfilled, there was a call for anyone else in the room to speak on behalf of the newly ordained man. Several people stood up and shared from their hearts about the ministry and dedication of the distinguished man.

Suddenly, without warning, the man that I had befriended and sat next to, stood up and addressed the crowd. He began to weep uncontrollably. After collecting himself, he said, "Because of this man, my son is in heaven. I cannot thank him enough for his willingness to share the gospel."

When the man sat back down, I leaned over and asked, "You've lost a son?" He and I shared a very rich time that day getting to know each other and bonding over our common circumstances. We may have appeared to overlook the fact that we're bonded as brothers in Christ, but we now found a fresh **belonging** in our grief and pain. Driving home, I couldn't stop thinking about the day. How was it possible that I would travel three and one-half hours away, sit in a room of 100 people whom I did not know, and the one person I would bond with shared the same circumstances as I did? *God, only You could do such things.*

Syrup

Psalm 13:1-2 (NIV), "How long, Lord? Will you forget me forever? How long will you hide your face from me? How long must I wrestle with my thoughts and day after day have sorrow in my heart? How long will my enemy triumph over me?"

I have been blessed by God with the aptitude to write. In fact, I have written more than one book. Because of God's great mercy, my first book was published, and I was even afforded the ability to travel on multiple occasions to promote it. While on the second leg of my book tour, Bob and I were traveling through Vermont on our way to another destination. Bob is a pastor friend of mine from Pennsylvania who I met on a retreat a few years ago. Bob wanted to help me distribute the book.

Unexpectedly, Bob yelled, "Stop! Pull over! This is the biggest syrup factory in North America. We must stop!" If you know Bob, you know that he is a bit peculiar, maybe even eccentric. So, it is not out of the ordinary for Bob to make such claims. In front of the large factory building stood a small, and designed to look old, log cabin. This log cabin was the gift shop.

As we walked up to the door, a woman in her late 50's walked out onto the porch and stated, "Thanks for coming gentlemen, but unfortunately, we have been closed since before COVID-19. We won't be opening for at least six more weeks. The best I can offer you today is a view through the window."

I had no interest in stopping anyway, so I began to look through my phone to catch up on emails and text messages. But that did not sit well with Bob. He began to browbeat this woman. Bob said, "You don't know how far we have traveled. You need to make an exception. I can't believe you would turn us away. You need to let us in." Suddenly, the voices were gone.

Not too much longer the woman peered her head out the door and said, "I have never had a man whine, cry, and beg like your friend. So, I let him in. You should probably come in as well." With that I entered.

Once inside, the woman gave us a tour of the place, and a history lesson on syrup. It was interesting, but not fascinating. Finally, the woman asked what we were doing and where we were going? I told her that I had written a book and Bob and I were out on a tour to promote the book. The woman asked what kind of book. I told her it was a book about faith and loving people, it was titled, "How Do I Love My Neighbor?" Immediately, I mean instantaneously, the woman's demeanor changed 180 degrees.

She almost screamed, "Don't you talk to me about God! I don't want to hear His name. You better stop while you're ahead. In fact, Leave! I want you gone right now! Get out!"

In the kindest and softest voice, I could muster, I asked, "Ma'am, can I ask why your behavior has so sharply hardened?"

At this she offered, "My daughter was murdered. The men who killed her are in prison for the rest of their miserable lives. I want them released. I want to kill them myself."

When I heard the pain in her voice, I reminded her that even if she were allowed to carry out her demands, it would never take her pain away. The pain she felt may soften over time, but it would never go away.

When she heard these words, she began to cry and said, "You don't know what it's like. The constant tearing at my soul, the ripping of my heart, the longing to hear her voice, to see her, to hold her. You could not possibly know what it's like."

I asked her name and then said, "Phil Ann, I could never know your pain. But I can relate in a small way. As I, too, have lost a child." At this, Phil Ann seemed to soften. The hardness she was previously wielding was gone. She even allowed me to share the things of God with her. We hugged and prayed together. I ministered to her. We cried and we laughed. We found ***belonging***. She gave me some syrup and I gave her a copy of my book. It was a much-needed time for both of us.

While driving away, Bob and I were trying to comprehend what we had just witnessed. How did God arrange such a meeting? What if Bob did not tell me to stop? What if Bob did not browbeat Phil Ann? What if she never asked what we were doing and where we were going? The list goes on and on. God, only You could do such things. *Only You, God, could allow two broken people to find peace and **belonging** amid brokenness.*

Funeral

Hebrews 13:2 (NIV), "Do not forget to show hospitality to strangers, for by so doing some people have shown hospitality to angels without knowing it."

Over the years, I have performed many funerals. Sometimes I am contacted directly. Other times I am referred by a church or a funeral home. I have even performed funeral services for some of the 52, mentioned earlier, that God has brought across my path. On this occasion, I was referred by a church. A man had died, and his family would gather to mourn him, as one would expect. Family members from different parts of the country came to pay their respects. This included the widow's adult daughter who had moved away many years prior because she married a man in the armed services. Because the family did not have strong church affiliation, they needed to find someone to guide them. So, the adult daughter contacted the church where she was baptized nearly 25 years earlier. That inquiry was passed on to me.

When I called the family and arranged a time for me to sit down with them (Saturday afternoon), the daughter decided to vet me to determine who I was. When she requested information from the only person with whom she still had ties to, at the church (after I called but before I arrived), that person stated that they did not know me. When I walked into the family's house, I was asked if I knew the person whom they were familiar with. I replied that I knew "of" that person but that I did not "know" them.

With arms folded, and sternness in her voice, the adult daughter stated, "That's right! I called my friend and he said he does not know you!" Seeing this, I wasn't sure if I was still wanted for the purposes for which they had reached out to the church.

There were many family members present, and we all sat down at the kitchen table. Then the widow asked me what my service looked like. I replied, "I usually begin with a poem."

The widow stated, "No! We are not doing that. What's next?"

I replied, "Then I share the specifics of the deceased (born on date/died on date, etc.)."

The widow stated, "No! We are not doing that. What's next?"

I replied, "Now we would pray to begin the service."

The widow stated, "You'll have to show me that because I am not sure we are doing that either." I asked that we all hold hands and I prayed for the family. At this, the widow stated, "Okay. I guess we can do that. What's next?"

I replied, "Now I will share some intimate details of your husband's life based on our conversation today." The widow stated, "No! We are not doing that. Everyone who knows him already knows the details of his life. Besides, many of our family members would like to speak and they will share those details. What's next?"

I replied, "I have a window in my service just for that reason, because usually there is someone who wants to share." The widow stated, "Good! Just to be clear, we are talking, and you are not. But you can introduce each of us as we speak. What's next?"

I replied, "Now we talk about your husband's faith." The widow stated, "No! We are not doing that either."

As you can imagine, this pre-funeral conversation is not going how I thought it was going to go. Then the widow asked again, "What's next?"

I replied, "Now I will share the gospel." The widow stated, "Which gospel will you be sharing?"

I replied, "The Good News." The widow stated, "No! We are not doing that. What's next?"

I replied, "Now we close in prayer." The widow stated, "You are not sharing one of your prayers. We have found a prayer in a book that we would like you to read." She pushed it in front of me and said, "Read it now."

The first line in the prayer read this way, "Do not grieve me." At this point I felt it necessary to interject in a more meaningful way. I said, "Ma'am, up to this point I have been extremely flexible and accommodating, I do not wish to be disrespectful. I am your servant and will do whatever is needed to provide a service for your husband that is honoring for all, but I must let you know that it is both unnatural and unhealthy to tell people not to grieve." That opened a long discussion about grief and the whole family joined in. It was decided that I would read the prayer from the book, minus the first sentence.

As I was putting my coat on to leave, the widow's brother and sister-in-law asked if they could have a few private moments with me before I left. I agreed. The sister-in-law stated with all the talk about grief and all the things they had learned, they felt trapped in limbo of the grief process. They felt as if they had not grieved properly. I asked, "How could I help?"

With tears in her eyes, the sister-in-law stated, "We lost our daughter 20 years ago and we don't know what to do." I opened my arms and hugged the woman. I embraced her long enough to include a whispered prayer in her ear. When we separated, the woman asked, "What just happened? I have never been embraced like that before."

To which I replied, "I have offered you the comfort from which I have received." The woman was confused and stated, "What does that mean?"

To which I replied, "I have walked in your shoes."

The woman cried even louder and asked, "You have lost a child as well?"

I replied, "Yes." Instantly, I went from being the guy who was met at the front door with crossed arms and stern voice as if to say, "we are not sure you **belong** here," to the guy everyone wanted around them. My status was changed because I **belonged** to a club that many run from like they run from lepers.

The next morning was the day of the service. The widow called me at 5:30 a.m. and stated, "I am so sorry that we dismantled your service. I've been giving it some thought, and I was wondering if you would share the piece about grief at the service today. I think it would be so helpful."

I replied, "Ma'am, I would be happy to do that for you."

She included this, "We are having a luncheon after the service, would you be our guest and join us?"

I replied, "Of course Ma'am. I would be delighted." At the luncheon, the widow sat at my left and the brother and sister-in-law sat on my right. We enjoyed each other's company and God had His way. You see, because I was not allowed, effectively prevented from sharing my service with this family, God intervened. *My **belonging** produced acceptance and the gospel was shared even though I did not say a word. Praise the Lord!*

Distinct

*1 Corinthians 9:19-23 (NIV), "Though I am free and **belong** to no one, I have made myself a slave to everyone, to win as many as possible. To the Jews I became like a Jew, to win the Jews. To those under the law I became like one under the law (though I myself am not under the law), so as to win those under the law. To those not having the law I became like one not having the law (though I am not free from God's law but am under Christ's law), so as to win those not having the law. To the weak I became weak, to win the weak. I have become all things to all people so that by all possible means I might save some. I do all this for the sake of the gospel, that I may share in its blessings."*

Like the Apostle Paul, who spiritedly attempted to become all things to all people to win as many as possible to the kingdom of God, essentially meeting people right where they are, I too have learned, by the grace of God, the value of meeting people right where they are. It's vitally important that we all learn to lessen our forwardness toward people and become more attuned to meeting their individual needs. Instead of giving the outpouring we want them to have, we should be more concerned with determining their needs and then meeting them. Of the 52 parents who God has brought to me, each of them has been distinctly different. If I would have, at any moment, been the least bit insensitive to their unique circumstances, I don't think I would have been chosen for this honor. You see, Paul did not pursue a self-chosen career. What Paul was given to steward he did not seek. His was both a revelation and a commission by God to plant churches and share the gospel with the Gentiles. Paul was apprehended! I certainly did not seek to lose a son. The 52 other parents that I have met thus far did not seek their loss either. I am quite certain no one does. Yet, in my case, and for far too many others, it has happened. Now I find myself in this position that I did not seek or pursue. Now I have an additional ministry, a calling, something additional to steward. It has brought me closer to God and it has planted my ***belonging*** deeper still.

When my son's death was still very raw and fresh, I had a moment with God like King David. After the infant son King David conceived with Bathsheba was found to be dead, King David got up off the floor and regained a sense of normal routine. I felt like God had asked me to get back into a normal routine as well. I didn't understand it, but I distinctly heard Him. At that time, I did not know there would be a running count of people that I would be asked to minister to. Some of the men that I spend time with on a consistent basis, got very angry and scolded me for displaying what they thought was a clear disrespect for my dead son, my family, and for decency in general. But they did not know, as I did not know, what God had in mind. As I previously stated, each of the 52 parents that I have met, all had different circumstances. How I would treat each of them and what I would do with each of them would be as different as their circumstances. Of the 52, I have been present at five of their children's funerals, two of them I performed.

In one instance, I would send the same text message that was sent to me on the day of my son's funeral, "I have a license to talk to you. Today I will begin praying for you. When you are ready, I will be here." Upon receiving this message, I was asked by the parents to please come and support them during their tragic day. We would spend much time that day comforting each other. In another instance, I remember sitting with a father, and the pain was so intense. He sticks out to me as someone who had lost everything, was totally bankrupt, wiped out, not knowing whether to keep living or to end his own life. His only child was gone. In 52 occurrences, I have never cried so hard and so long with anyone else. We shared very few words, but we spent hours in each other's company. In both funerals that I performed, neither family knew walking into the start of our relationship that I had walked in their shoes. I always like to sit with any family prior to a funeral I perform. I want to make sure that I have enough information about their loved one and can share from a place of confidence, not of vacancy. In these moments prior to the funeral, sitting with the families who had lost a child, when it was discovered, we were connected, that we ***belonged***, they were more receptive and vulnerable. We shared our tears, and it was beautiful.

I have had some further contact with many of the 52. Some, more than others. But because each one is different; I try to respect their space. Some things that I have never said to any of the 52 include, "I know how you feel," and, "This is what you should do." I may have walked in their shoes, but their circumstances, their relationships with their deceased child, and their pain is distinctly different. So, I have tried very hard to steward well what God has given to me. On this side of heaven, I may never know why He chose me. However, as I have stated before, *drawing closer to God only serves to strengthen my **belonging**.*

-Lessons Learned-

In the most tragic moments of our lives, God is still with us. The pain and anguish we experience can cause us to miss out on the blessings of God. It would be easy to allow our tragedy to create a barrier to everyone around us, but sometimes it is a bridge to connect us to others. If we are willing, God can and will take even those moments that we want to forget and leverage them for His glory. He calls into being something that did not previously exist and **belonging** appears from nothing.

Lord, help me to remember who You have created me to be. Never let me forget that I belong to You. My true identity is found in You, for I am Your child—a beautiful masterpiece. You delight in me. (Author Unknown)

4

Searching, Longing, Hoping

Psalm 119:82 (TPT), 'I'm consumed with longings for your promises, so I ask, "When will they all come true?" '

Within any family, there always exists the desire to know where we fit, if we are appreciated, what is my value, do I *belong*? This desire never leaves us, for we were created to be together and to receive love and affection. This longing to *belong* is innate. Some people are exceptionally alert and willing to continuously offer the answers to these questions through praise, encouragement, and love. They are the parents who understand that their children are blessings from God. I am not attempting to conclude that the parents who aren't good at offering encouragement to their children don't love them. I am simply stating that some parents do an amazing job at nurturing their children's value and providing a sense of *belonging*. Did the parents that do a great job at encouraging their children receive the same encouragement from their own parents? Perhaps. But not necessarily. All parents have the same choices in front of them. Will I take the best things that I received from my parents and offer them to my children? Will I be intentional enough to change or remove the things that I did not find valuable from my childhood for my children's sake? Will I throw caution to the wind and not really give any great thought to how I will raise my children? The list goes on.

Parenting is challenging, demanding, draining, and hard. Parenting is also tremendously rewarding and is a delight as we watch our children grow and develop. Each day brings new joys and hardships as we navigate through the seasons of our children's growth. But what happens when we make our lives more complicated? What happens when we find our marriages falling apart? What happens when we attempt to bridge two fragmented families together? Our world is experiencing broken families at rates beyond comprehension.

The divorce rate for first time marriages is above 50 percent. Worse yet, the divorce rate for second marriages is above 75 percent. With so many families in a state of confusion, trying to sustain, and hemorrhaging in chaos, how would anyone, let alone the children, know that they **belong**?

This problem our world is experiencing is beyond any one person's ability to grasp. The totality of brokenness that we are producing through divorce and blending of families is staggering. One might say that more than half of our families are being killed. What are we willing to do about this epidemic? If a "disease" was killing half the people on the planet, great lengths would be taken by all forms of government and leadership to combat it. Many parents just don't understand the severity of what is at stake when they make decisions (to divorce or to blend a family) that affect their family, not just themselves. This book is not about marriage or blended families. This book is about **belonging**, and the power **belonging** has to produce wholeness and contentment. However, the direct result from both entities (divorce and blended family) strips people, especially children, of their innate desire to **belong**.

I also would like to make another point as clear as I can; not all families suffer the same. Some learn to thrive despite these less-than-ideal circumstances. But the majority of families and children suffer great loss. When my parents divorced, there probably weren't a lot of books to read, seminars to sit through, or even counselors to visit, to help them understand their circumstances. Divorce has been around for a long time, but back then, more than 48 years ago, it was not as prevalent as it is today. My parents married young. They were 18, and I was on the way, which probably precipitated their decision to marry. Maybe they thought it was the right thing to do at the time? Their marriage scarcely lasted 10 years. My brothers and I have lived in a state of confusion since then.

Our parents stole our **belonging** and did not know how to instill that state-of-being in us thereafter. Please don't think that I am here to bash my parents. They were kids having kids. And like most people, when things got tough, they ran away from their problems, or so they thought. I hope to be crystal clear with my next statement. Marriage is hard; divorce is hard; choose your hard. What most families are finding out today is that divorce is *"the gift"* that keeps on giving. You can't run from it, especially where children are involved. After 48 years of living in the aftermath of my parent's divorce, my brothers and our families are still feeling the ill effects of their decision to divorce. Although my brothers and I have managed to reduce the level of dysfunction and chaos in our individual families, living mostly well-adjusted lives, our parents have never made it easy for us to thrive. They didn't know how, and never learned to provide anything remotely close to **belonging**. Sadly, neither did any of our parent's new spouses. The value of family and the importance of both the mother and the father in the home is more important than anyone could ever appreciate.

To provide some clarity into my family tree, please follow along. My father and mother married and had three children, Jeff, Bob, and James. After my parents divorced from each other, they each remarried two more times. My mother's second marriage was to a man named Dominic. Dominic had two daughters, Denise, and Colleen, prior to marrying my mother. Denise and Colleen became our stepsisters through marriage. My mother and Dominic produced no children of their own. My father's second marriage was to a woman named Jan. Jan had no children prior to their marriage. My father and Jan produced no children of their own. My mother's third marriage was to a man named Harrold. Harrold had no children prior to marrying my mother. She and Harrold produced no children of their own. My father's third marriage was to a woman named Cindy. Cindy had no children of her own prior to marrying my father. She and my father produced two children, Lindsey, and Stephanie. Lindsey and Stephanie are mine and my brother's sisters. Denise and Colleen at one point were our stepsisters until the divorce of their father and my mother. My father has a total of five children from two marriages. My mother has three children total.

What my parents failed to grasp, and what most parents who entertain divorce and blending of families also neglect to realize is that, as the parent(s), you made the choice for everyone else. I don't want to discount the desire and need to be together with someone, but taking broken families and bringing them together is serious business. If a person dents the hood of their car, there is a body shop close by that will repair the dent. The hood will then appear to be perfect or unblemished, but that is an illusion, because there is no way to return the hood to its former state. It has been repaired. When you bridge two broken families with multiple personalities, there is no illusion big enough for the family to appear repaired. Being a blended family parent is arguably the hardest job on the planet.

If parents understood that, they might be more likely to work through their problems with their original spouse and refrain from entering the blended family space. Long ago, there was a television show called "I Love Lucy." In one episode, Lucille Ball was depicted as a chocolatier working in a candy shop. There is a scene where Lucy is standing at the end of a conveyor belt and pieces of chocolate are falling on the floor because Lucy cannot gather the chocolate pieces fast enough. The scene is very funny, until you view it through the lens of a metaphor for the parent of a blended family. Suddenly, the humor is gone, and the extreme challenges emerge. That is what it's like every day for a parent of a blended family.

Years ago, I was working for a company that was hired to install an assembly line in an auto plant. There were multiple components and operations integrated in the line. Through trial and error, it was discovered that one of the operations had been mismanaged. No matter how many times we tried and no matter how many workers we brought in to complete the operation, it would not function as intended. The window of operation was 12 seconds, but it took 15 seconds to complete it. Everyone knew that the operation was going to be revisited and corrected. But the person stationed at this site knew that every day until it was corrected, they would never catch a breath, never get a break, never complete the task, and never leave work with a sense of job well done. The chocolate was coming down the conveyor belt faster than anyone could catch it. Again, this is what it's like every day as a parent in a blended family.

I believe it's necessary to state again, to re-illuminate the point that, as the parent, you chose this. At first, most parents believe they can handle the problems that arise. What they can't see and what they don't know is that the problems continue to arise and change in complexity. What happens to many parents is that they begin to regret the choice they made. This regret deepens as time goes on and the parents become less likely to want to cover the bases, to provide for the needs of their children, and to solve the problems. Who tends to suffer more when the problems continue to occur? The children do. The children who did not make the decision to attempt to bridge two broken families into one happy family. Children are not inanimate objects, like the hood of a car, that can be repaired under the illusion that it has been restored to its former state. The children were not consulted when the decision was made to get the divorce and break up their biological family. Nor were the children consulted when the decision was made to entertain a blended family. The children all have needs, wants, personalities, and problems that must be attended to. Nevertheless, most parents in this environment never seem to have the foresight to count the cost. Additionally, the problems of the divorce both parents thought they left behind only adds to the problems they are facing every day.

My parents are still dealing with the complexities of their decision to choose to divorce 48 years ago. The bigger concern in my family is that there are more than 20 family members (children/spouses/grandchildren) still being directly affected because of the poor choices two people (my mother and father) made 48 years ago. The negative consequences of *divorce* continue to happen. And the **belonging** for most of the people in my family is still evading them.

Favoritism

James 2:8-9 (NIV), 'If you really keep the royal law found in Scripture, "Love your neighbor as yourself," you are doing right. But if you show favoritism, you sin and are convicted by the law as lawbreakers.'

My brothers and I were still very young (12, 10, and 6) when my mother married her second husband. I have so many memories that are still so vivid. We had good times, but some were not so good. My mother's second husband had two daughters; one was two years my junior, the other two years my senior. But from the moment my mother married her second husband, my father would make declarations to my brothers and I when we visited him on the weekends. These declarations were sternly commanded to us by our father every time we saw him, and they lasted for months. I could only imagine that he made such statements because his second marriage was to a woman who had no children, nor did he have additional children with her.

Perhaps, the thought of introducing new children into the mix was too much for him. I don't have any other logical reason that would make sense for why my father acted in the way that he did. The statements he made repeatedly were as follows, "These girls are not your sisters! They will never be your sisters! They will never be your family! Don't you dare include them in any way!" Remember, my brothers and I were still very young, and these statements were hard to receive. But this was our dad, and we were clinging to any sense of *belonging* we could at the time.

To be fair, my mother's second husband did not provide any relief to my father's statements. Whenever his daughters were in our company, they were treated like precious dolls that would easily break if you were too careless with them. It was as if my brothers and I were the grunts, or the slaves, and his daughters were royalty or celebrities. This unfair dichotomy never changed the entire time my mother was married to this man. I remember once, while on vacation, all five kids went swimming even though we were not supposed to. Because we were wet and not in bathing suits, my mother's husband pulled his belt out and my brothers and I became the example of his fury because we were disobedient. However, his daughters were never touched. He did not even raise his voice to them. Perhaps he was attempting to maintain peace and good consistent contact with his own children because they were only with us every other weekend. My brothers and I were in a constant search for *belonging* because our parents seemed to be oblivious to our needs.

Almost a year after my mother married her second husband, his daughter, my youngest stepsister was at our house visiting. Her sister did not come on this occasion. My brothers and I were about to be picked up by our dad, and it was suggested, by my stepfather, that she should tag along with us. This suggestion was made from necessity as there was going to be nothing for her to do as my brothers and I would not be there to keep her company. As we started to drive away with my father, he decided that this little girl needed a new outfit, and we would spend our time that day finding the perfect one for her. As we spent hours between two different malls attempting to find just the right outfit for this girl, my brothers and I kept making eye contact between ourselves. We never said a word about it to each other until years later. But our thoughts were of hurt, sadness, profound confusion, and even abandonment. Why would our dad make these continuous, stern, and dividing statements about these two girls and then drag us along with him to shop for her? It made no sense to us. Who did we *belong* to?

The entanglement we had with these two girls would carry on long after my mother and their father would divorce. During my mother's marriage to this man (second husband), my own father disliked him, you might even say that he hated him. That is until my mother's divorce from her second husband was final. Then my own father seemed to have a totally different view of this man. He sympathized with him and seemed to want to be his friend. The whole thing was very confusing for me and my brothers. But like I said, this was our lot. These moments were constant, almost "normal."

Fast forward nearly 20 years. My father is now living in a new neighborhood with his third wife. My brothers and I, with our families are going to visit because there was some sort of celebration. I cannot explain the absolute perplexity my mind was caught in when I arrived at his house to find the older of the two daughters from my mother's second marriage in my father's house. She and her husband were now my father's neighbors, and apparently friends. I don't want to create an impression that my father can't have whatever friends he wants or spend time with whomever he chooses, but remember, my father spent months convincing us that we should not get close to these girls. He went out of his way to speak unkind words toward their father for years while my mother and he were married. My father never explained himself or ever offered an explanation.

After the party was over, I approached my father to inquire about the person(s) in his house. When I mentioned my confusion, he became very angry and said, "Don't you ever tell me who my friends can be!"

I replied, "Dad, I was just trying to understand, to see what you see. You have never shared an explanation for why you were so indifferent towards them years ago. I am just trying to understand. That's all."

His reply was, "My friends are my friends, and you don't concern yourself." This moment for me was very perplexing because of the history involved. My *belonging* was also in question.

Years later, at my younger sister Stephanie's wedding, my brothers and I arrived at the hall with our own families and were surprised to find our seats located in the farthest corner from the head table. Where we were sitting might not have been so bad, until a closer look would reveal that my former stepsisters, my mother's second husband's daughters, were sitting in front of the head table. The same girls that had entered our lives nearly four decades earlier, the same girls whom my father slandered, the same girls whom my father said would never be our sisters, these same girls were seated in a place where my brothers and I should have been seated. It begs the question; do these girls **belong** to my father or do my brothers and I **belong** to my father?

Wounded

Colossians 3:21 (NIV), "Fathers, do not embitter your children, or they will become discouraged."

For my entire junior year and most of my senior year of high school I lived with my father. I always felt like I needed to be closer to my father. My mother was never willing to let me go live with him. I finally convinced her to let me go the summer before my junior year. I remember thinking that my sense of **belonging** would finally be established because I was now close to my father, no longer was I seeing him every other weekend. Our relationship seemed to grow stronger during this time of my life. I am not sure that I had everything worked out in my head, but it felt like we were definitely moving in the right direction. I grew up with two cousins the same age, Greg and Keith, and we all attended the same school. Everyone knows when certain kids get together there is always some sort of trouble. This was the case for me and both of my cousins. I don't think I would call us troublemakers, but we would tend to do things we knew we shouldn't do. One day, in the high school parking lot, Keith and I were in Greg's car. Why we decided to rip up his schoolbooks I will never know, but that is exactly what we did. When Greg returned to his car and saw what we had done, he turned us into the principal.

I was suspended for three days from high school. I felt horrible, confused, ashamed, and slightly depressed. I thought, how could I have been so stupid? When I was sent home the next day, my father phoned me from work during his lunch break. I expected a stern talking to. I expected a lecture. I also expected some form of punishment in the form of strong disciplinary action. What I didn't expect is what I received that day. The words my father shared with me that day were very damaging to my **belonging**. Sadly, I would carry them with me as my identity for far too many years. I am sure he was very disappointed with me and probably not thinking clearly. Remember, we had not lived together for nearly 10 years prior to this season of our lives. We were probably just more than a year together at this time. This was probably his first real opportunity to discipline me.

When I got on the phone, these were the words my father shouted at me, "Jeffrey, you are a piece of shit! You are not worth the ground I walk on! I am calling your mother and your ass will be gone by the end of the day. I am done with you." As horrible as I felt about the incident that caused this disruption, nothing could have prepared me for the flood of emotions that washed over me in that moment. I was lost, broken, and crushed. The hurt that ensued cannot be described. My longing to ***belong*** was thrown away like chaff in the wind.

Over the years my father and I have had several opportunities to revisit this moment in our lives. What became normal, is that he never failed to point out something that I fell short on, reminding me that I was not good enough. In those moments I would remind him of his horrible words spoken to me in his house that day. Every time this conversation would come up, he would deny it ever happened or simply say he doesn't remember it that way. For the next 30-plus years I heard the same denial from him, never acknowledging, never apologizing, never taking responsibility, always blowing it off. My father wasted no time pointing out everyone else's flaws, but he could never admit fault of his own. In fact, there are two words my father has never shared with me or my brothers.... "I'm sorry." We never heard anything that resembled "please forgive me," or "that did not come out right," or "my apologies," or "my bad," or "my fault," or "I take responsibility," or "I didn't mean for that to happen," or "oops." My father knew how to point his finger in other people's direction, but he never managed to point it at himself.

Then one night something unusual happened. My father and I were attempting to understand each other through a series of lunches and dinners. We were sitting down at a table in a restaurant and my father proceeded to denigrate my brothers. This was his usual way of entering into a new conversation with me. To this day, whenever I enter my father's presence, he throws insults at and belittles, my brothers. It's almost as if he's telling me in an odd way that I am his favorite. This is problematic on two levels. First, why does he think this is appropriate behavior? Who demeans their own children? Who demeans their own children in front of their other children? My father has done this for as long as I can remember. Second, whichever brother is in his presence, the two remaining brothers are his targets for cruel and disgusting accusations.

However, on this night, my father did not demean what my brothers did, but levied accusations about what they had said. To this, I reminded him that he is "that" same person. I told my father, "If you have ever said something negative or insensitive about someone, anyone, then you cannot point your finger at anyone else because you are just as guilty." As I expected, my father quickly defended his position. It's worth noting, self-protection always places the relationship at a far distant second. I know this today but did not know it then. When he sternly defended himself again, and stated he had never done such a thing, I reminded him of his words to me some 35 years earlier.

I was very surprised when he did not shrug it off, when he did not try to pretend it never happened, or that he doesn't remember. On this night, he looked at me and said, "You deserved what I said back then." I remember being a bit shocked by his response but elated at the same time.

I said to my father, "It only took 35 years, but tonight we have graduated to a new level of maturity. Now, all I will ask you to do, dad, as the father of five, is remove Bob and James' names from your accusations and replace them with the names Lindsey and Stephanie. Are you willing to say the same things and act with the same veracity towards your daughters? Or do you only reserve those ugly thoughts for your sons?"

At this he stopped talking. This is exactly what my father does whenever he is questioned about inappropriate behavior. Our evening ended, he never responded one way or the other, and my ***belonging*** remained where it has always been, "drifting in the wind."

Trash

James 3:9-10 (NIV), "With the tongue we praise our Lord and Father, and with it we curse human beings, who have been made in God's likeness. Out of the same mouth come praise and cursing. My brothers and sisters, this should not be."

During one of the many seasons of quiet in my family, something most unusual occurred. My brother James had been divorced from his second wife, Michelle, for only a short time. While Michelle was out dining at a local restaurant, she was surprised to run into my father and stepmother Cindy. They approached Michelle as they entered the restaurant and entertained her with some small talk until their table was ready. Michelle was a bit taken back that they would approach her because they had very little to do with her for the nine years she was married to my brother. To give context to this, Michelle had four children of her own and when my brothers and our families would get together, it seemed to bother my father that we would spend time together. He once said to me, "I don't know why you are including her and her children, they are not part of this family."

I reminded my father that because of marriage, they were family, and we will include them always. Having grown up in the same type of environment as her children, wondering where I *belong*, my brothers and I probably went out of our way to include them.

My father and stepmother concluded their meal quickly and found Michelle still sitting and enjoying her dining experience. So, they decided to sit down and share some more conversation. At some point, shortly thereafter, my father and stepmother invited Michelle and her children to their house for dinner. That seemed quite strange to Michelle, but she kept talking with them. Then Michelle asked, "In my nine years of marriage to your son, I never quite understood the conflict between you and your boys. Can you help me understand what I am missing?"

That's when my father and stepmother said this, "We're done with those boys. We threw them out like trash." Even though Michelle was my brother's ex-wife, she had a really hard time swallowing the words that she had just heard. When she left the restaurant, she reached out to my brother and shared with him the hurtful things that she heard. I am not sure why she called my brother that night. Maybe she wanted to apologize for not understanding his struggle with his father? Maybe she just wanted to stir the pot? In the end, it really does not matter because my father would back her story but not without some prodding first.

When James shared with me what Michelle had said to him, I reached out to my father. I said, "Dad, I just heard something that I think we should talk about." So, I shared the words with him that Michelle had heard him say. At first, he said he didn't know what I was talking about. To that I said, "Dad, this is a pretty specific choice of words. It seems odd that someone would make this up. Are you sure you have no idea?"

Then my father said, "It was really loud in the restaurant, I could barely hear anything at all."

I responded, "Dad, which is it? You couldn't hear? Or, you have no idea what I am talking about?"

Then my father said, "Cindy and Michelle were talking but I could not hear."

When he didn't deny saying the words that I had confronted him with, I pressed even further. To this my father said, "I'm sure some things were said, but I can't remember everything, besides I couldn't hear."

At this, I asked, "Dad, how could this happen? How does a parent tell anyone that they threw their child in the trash? How do these words come out of your mouth? What have we done to deserve this? Did you somehow think you were in a safe space, with your son's ex-wife, so you could say whatever you wanted and get away with it?" When my father became frustrated, he finally admitted to saying the words.

He said, "You guys deserve it." What didn't follow this exchange, what has never followed any exchange my father and I have ever had, is an apology. It's hard to feel like you **belong** when your father and his wife will tell people they threw you in the trash.

Waiting

Romans 5:5 (NIV), "And hope does not put us to shame, because God's love has been poured out into our hearts through the Holy Spirit, who has been given to us."

My father has three sons from his first marriage and two daughters from his third marriage. We have never been one family; we have always been fragmented as two separate families. As a result, the sons, and the daughters, (brothers and sisters) have never really been close. There have been some brief moments where everything appeared to be solid, but if you really knew us, you would know it was all a façade of my father's making. Whether he was unwilling to blend us, or didn't know how to blend us, he, the father, was the one who invited us all into this dilemma. He was the leader of the family.

Because my sisters have never lived in a divorced household, my brothers and I could never hold them accountable for our lack of unity or attachment. They had never been made to travel back and forth between mom and dad's house, never been forced to listen to one parent verbally assault the other, never been forced to write a letter to the Friend of the Court. They had never been introduced to people who pretended to be their family because mom or dad remarried only to find out at holidays, funerals, and weddings they were not really family at all. All the *"invisibly silent"* and *"emotionally-damaging"* things that happen to children when their parents decide to break up, my sisters had never participated in, so they had no perspective. There was no way for them to understand. In fact, my father, having never blended us, afforded my sisters a life of consistency. They had the luxury of living "normal" and occasionally, there would be a brother or two to spend a few hours with. Did my sisters know that their brothers didn't **belong**?

My brothers and I made many attempts to bridge our family(s), but never with any help from our father. The obstacles we faced were always the same. First, those who lived in my father's house were never concerned with blending us, because for them, life was normal. It was as though they were saying to my brothers and I, "Why would we want to repair something that isn't broken?" Those living in my father's house always wanted to look good for the picture moments of life, so there was always a fuss for my brothers and I to show up when it counted. But for the everyday normal routines of life, we didn't seem to matter to them. Second, no one else knew the experience of being on the outside looking in. Nobody else knew what it was like to be the children in a divorce.

Apart from my father who divorced my mother, nobody ever experienced the unpleasantries of divorce the way my brothers and I had. Even after my sisters were married, whenever we would attempt to talk about the subject as a group, nobody else had any experience. Of the five children, their spouses, and my father and stepmother, only three people could possibly understand what it felt like standing on the outside looking in. Somehow that didn't prevent 12 opinions from being shared. Eventually, mine and my brothers' individual families were negatively affected and wounded by the seeming lack of empathy from these circumstances. Actually, it was more like a callous dismissal of attention.

After my sisters had their own children, something started to shift. They began to see a larger picture, one where family and togetherness, and connectedness was important. When all five siblings decided to sit down and make a serious attempt at being a family, a real family, there was great hope in the air. However, my youngest brother, James, was not so quick to come to the table. He had serious reservations and was not sure he wanted to open himself up to the possibility of further hurt and rejection. After I encouraged him to please join us, he cautiously did. I was so grateful that we had finally arrived at what looked like a real chance at true harmony. Many times, just thinking about it, I was brought to tears. We were on the cusp of real *belonging*.

When we sat down for the first time, there was a lot of discussion directed towards the willingness to see the other side. We all knew this was going to be a monumental task. We weren't sure whether our father was going to be a help or a hindrance. We all had spouses and children and all of them had their own ideas of what they wanted because of the pain, frustration, and separation that had been inflicted on our family for so many years. Because of all the moving parts, the five siblings made an agreement that we would stick together and fight for unity, that we would do whatever it took to be unified.

It was in that moment that my brother James said something that turned out to be prophetic. What he said was true, but none of us really knew how wise his statement was. We all realized later, especially after everything came crumbling down. James looked at our sisters and said, "I feel sorry for you girls. Jeff, Bob, and I have been made to make constant adjustments and compromises, to accept things we didn't want to, to learn and grow in ways that we weren't supposed to, but we had to anyway. We have been conditioned by circumstances that we never created. You, on the other hand, have been living in a different world. That is not your fault. But the decisions in front of you will be more challenging than you could possibly imagine. You may have to walk in defiance of your parents for the benefit of this group. Choices that we have been facing for decades, you will face for the first time. I don't think you know what you are entering into with this agreement."

Both girls said they were ready and willing. We all left that meeting with great hope. And at first, things were great. There was a real commitment from all five of us, our spouses, and our children. We were finally on our way. As you might expect, we all began to see differently what we could not see previously.

One day, my sister Stephanie asked my brother Bob why James was so reticent towards our father and held onto so much anger. Bob asked Stephanie, "Have you ever been on vacation with dad?"

Stephanie, now in her early thirties, replied, "Yes, every year since I was born and sometimes twice a year."

Bob asked, "Would it be fair to say that you have taken a vacation with our father 50 times in your life?"

Stephanie responded, "Yes, that sounds about right."

Bob asked, "How many times do you think James has been on vacation with our father?"

Stephanie said, "I don't know."

Bob stated, "James has been on exactly zero vacations with our father. You have been on 50 vacations with our father. James is 50 years old and has never been on vacation with our father. Why do you think James carries so much anger and hurt? The lack of a vacation is just one element of James' life. If we were to examine every aspect of his life and compare it to yours, how many other discrepancies do you think we might find? Do you think that is fair? Do you now begin to see why we have been desiring and probing for fairness and ***belonging***?"

After hearing more detailed stories of our lives and seeing and understanding with greater clarity, our relationships were growing deeper and more meaningful. We were fond of each other and trusting each other just like one would think a brother and sister should. One day Stephanie and I were talking on the phone, and she began to share more intimate details with me. She shared some of the experiences that had occurred in her life and how they had negatively affected not only her, but also her husband and her children. There were moments where her husband removed them completely from the presence of my father and stepmother because of their behavior. She started realizing more and more that the experiences my brothers and I were sharing because of our father's behavior were happening to her as well, albeit less severely and less frequently.

Then she said something that I will never forget. Because she now had children of her own and could understand what it's like to demonstrate a protective love for them, she made this statement, "As I stare into the faces of these two beautiful little girls, I ask myself, under what circumstances would I be willing to both say and do the things to them that I have witnessed our father say and do to you. For the life of me, I cannot come up with one."

I replied, "Stephanie, you will never say and do such things to your daughters. I am so thankful that you now have the perspective to see that. But now I want you to imagine how long the season was for James, Bob, and I. We have had to wait more than 30 years for you to gain that experience and all the while we never held you accountable because it wasn't your fault." The pause on the phone was beyond uncomfortable. For the first time, Stephanie was truly beginning to see the depth and totality of what her brothers had been saying for so long. She could now begin to see our fight for **belonging**.

Brothers

Proverbs 17:17 (NIV), "A friend loves at all times, and a brother is born for a time of adversity."

The following story is my brother James' memory of how his hope of **belonging** will always remain a mystery. When we read a person's thoughts, what is the first thing that comes to our minds? Do we offer a space for compassion, knowing that there is pain in their words? Or do we offer apathy because we think they should just get over it? The answer will always lie in the way we view their circumstances. Do we only perceive it from our own perspective, or do we attempt to view it from their perspective?

{James' story}

The feeling of **belonging** has remained an illusion my entire life. I have many reasons for saying this but the feeling like I never had a home stands out as the most significant. My parents divorced when I was two years old. As a result, they were never able to provide stability or comfort for me.

Growing up, I was never with my father for any longer than a weekend at a time. Many times, I was away from my mother's house as well, as she often pushed me off to my aunt's (her sister) house for days at a time. During my mother's second marriage I never felt safe at mom's house as it was run by a tyrant, my stepfather. He was the man who raised me, and his method was an iron fist. When he got angry, I often felt his actual fist. Although my mother knew all along and did nothing to change it, the iron fist ran that house until I left after graduating high school. It was then that I finally built up the courage and ran out of the house. I told my mother, "I will never ever go back in." She and her second husband were in marriage trouble by then, so it wasn't long after that the tyrant moved on. I returned when he left. Shortly after their divorce, my mother brought her third husband around. However, it didn't take long for him to convince her that I needed to be gone.… my mother seemed to have no hesitations. In anger, we parted ways.

In my dark moments growing up, I was looking to find that sense of security from someone. So, I turned to my father for support. I remember running to my father crying out for help. Unfortunately, he would always tell me "No" and then return me right back to my mother's unprotected home. My father knew what was happening there but showed no concern for my safety. His focus and energy were always spent in the direction of his third wife and their two children. My father not only turned a blind eye to my life at my mother's house, but even the time we spent together on weekends seemed like we weren't together. There was no feeling of security or acceptance… I never felt like I *belonged*.

Both of my parents were far too busy with their lives to notice me. I found myself acting out in hopes of being noticed by the people who were supposed to be there for me, my parents. They only saw it as me being a troubled teen. I am now 50 and a lot has happened. I still hold a lot of resentment toward those people who did not care for me. I find myself bitter toward them because of our past. I have yet to find that feeling of *belonging* because I was never shown how. Without feeling their love and support I find myself in a place of unknowing. Unknowing of what it's like to be supported by the two people who gave me life. Unknowing of what stability looks like because of all the people who came in and out of my life for short periods of time. And unknowing what it is like to trust others who say they are family. All these things seem like an illusion to me.

The only two people I have been able to count on my whole life are my older brothers. Not only have we shared the trauma of growing up in similar circumstances with our parents, but they have been my "rock" for the last 50 years. They have shown me what it's like to be loved and how to trust others. It took me a while to find that. Whatever the feeling of truly *belonging* is, it has always eluded me. Today, my parents no longer have such a strong hold on me. I have learned that a title is just a title. It's just a word. Unfortunately, I no longer have a relationship with my parents. Each day I focus on trying to build better relationships with the people who are in my life. Maybe one day I'll find a place where I do *belong*, a place where I feel at home…

-Lessons Learned-

We live in a throwaway society. If something is broken, we think, "let's just replace it." When we live in this environment long enough, it can affect every thought we have, including those that involve our marriage. When we complicate our lives by getting divorced, we must learn that our problems will also become more prevalent. Many of us believe that all our problems will go away when we divorce, but all we really managed to do was create a new setting where our problems will follow us, sometimes forever. *Belonging*, which was supposed to be for our good, has now become a battlefield that frequently leaves us wounded and bruised instead. The trail of generational curses we are leaving behind us because of divorce is staggering. Knowing better should result in doing better. May we learn to make better choices so *belonging* prevails.

Identity Matters

Psalm 24:1 (TPT), "Yahweh claims the world as his. Everything and everyone belong to him!"

5

Family United?

By this point in my life, I had spent decades trying to gain understanding of how and why my family was structured in brokenness. I longed for answers that had yet to be revealed and desperately wanted to find the *belonging* that had eluded me for so many years. Would we ever be united? Would I ever find my *belonging*? God continued to mature me along the way and placed people in my life to bring clarity. Many spiritual fathers deposited much needed discernment, understanding, and wisdom within me. With clarity comes patience and the willingness to allow God to have His way. We no longer need to see the evidence of our labor, nor are we concerned with the outcome. God had grown me to a level of maturity where I could finally see that I had been attempting to force my desired result of unity out of my family's brokenness. Be careful what you ask for, God might just give it to you.

With the leadership propensity to be able to see from multiple perspectives, such a person must be willing to demonstrate both the walk and the talk. I asked God for clarity, and He gave me discernment and wisdom to see what I could not see previously. But that made my interactions with my family much more difficult because now grace was more important than ever. Now I realized that I needed God more than I ever did before. God gave me the opportunity to see through my own words that where I was about to trek was more difficult.

I remember asking a man some questions after his mother's funeral. What was ironic, is that those questions eventually became the very words that God would lay on my heart in terms of my family struggles. During the COVID-19 pandemic I was asked to perform a funeral. Even though it was family only, because of COVID-19, there were 12 adult children and their spouses, plus grandchildren and great-grandchildren. This was not a small crowd by any means. After the service was complete, one of the adult sons approached me and wanted to talk about something that was troubling him. He said, "I feel like I can talk to you. In case you didn't know, or haven't figured it out yet, I am a gay man. My problem is that I cannot find acceptance in this world, I can't even find it right here in this room within my family." He proceeded to share with me how he was giving kindness, and treating people with respect, and loving people, but no matter what he does, he cannot gain acceptance from his family. He ended with this phrase, "I just don't **belong** here."

Not knowing his family history, I could only comment on what he had just said to me. So, I stated, "Sir, it sounds like you have deep understanding. It sounds like you have excellent discernment. It sounds like you know better. But if all that is true, are you then telling me that your posture is arms wide open displaying acceptance and love to everyone no matter what? If so, I have two questions for you. How long will you hold that posture? Will you keep your arms open until everyone else comes to the same understanding as you have?"

The man paused for a long while and then said, "That seems really hard, almost impossible."

I replied, "Yes, it is. It's extremely hard. But if we are going to say we know better, then we must be willing to demonstrate that we know better. If not, we have only managed to display hypocrisy. We are, in fact, worse than the person we are confronting."

Romans 2:1-5 (NIV), "You, therefore, have no excuse, you who pass judgment on someone else, for at whatever point you judge another, you are condemning yourself, because you who pass judgment do the same things. Now we know that God's judgment against those who do such things is based on truth. So when you, a mere human being, pass judgment on them and yet do the same things, do you think you will escape God's judgment? Or do you show contempt for the riches of his kindness, forbearance and patience, not realizing that God's kindness is intended to lead you to repentance? But because of your stubbornness and your unrepentant heart, you are storing up wrath against yourself for the day of God's wrath, when his righteous judgment will be revealed."

That's when my words started to haunt me. I thought, leaders and "agents of change" do not spread hypocrisy and division, they spread the message of hope, even in the face of opposition. My desire for family unity and for **belonging** would have to wait. I would have to offer even more grace while waiting for the rest of my family to want the same unity that I had wanted for so long. Even though my father was supposed to be the leader, I cannot assume that he knows how to lead, especially since he had walked himself into, arguably, the most difficult environment on the planet. If he did in fact know how, perhaps we would not be so fragmented. I certainly cannot blame my sisters or their husbands as none of them had grown up in divorce. They have no perspective of my circumstances. Neither could I cast blame on my stepmother, as she also had no perspective. I didn't know how I would demonstrate the righteousness that I wanted to see in my family, while sitting in the longsuffering of waiting.

Ecclesiastes 1:18 (NIV), "For with much wisdom comes much sorrow; the more knowledge, the more grief."

More conversations were needed between family members. More willingness from every person to want unity was necessary. There was usually apprehension from every person in mine and my brother's families. They all felt stuck and lacked **belonging** because of our fragmented, unblended *mess*. However, we were willing to move forward if something new was on the menu, if some changes for the better were going to occur. We had all walked this road of empty promises and lack of change so many times before and it always ended ugly. To rip off the scabs and open the wounds of the past with nothing new to provide hope was never easy. This was the pattern my father's household seemed to enjoy. But it never fared well because the circumstances were never viewed through the lens of the person(s) that lacked **belonging**. We always ended up right where we started. At this point, that was all I could do, hope for something new.

Plagued

Psalm 91:1-6 (NIV), 'Whoever dwells in the shelter of the Most High will rest in the shadow of the Almighty. I will say of the Lord, "He is my refuge and my fortress, my God, in whom I trust." Surely he will save you from the fowler's snare and from the deadly pestilence. He will cover you with his feathers, and under his wings you will find refuge; his faithfulness will be your shield and rampart. You will not fear the terror of night, nor the arrow that flies by day, nor the pestilence that stalks in the darkness, nor the plague that destroys at midday.'

Even with all the momentum we had going for us and all the greatest intentions, we were still not making all the progress we had hoped to make. My father and stepmother were slow to respond to everything that was happening around them. They both were caught off guard when their daughters began to make plans that did not include them. They were also hearing statements from their daughters that did not line up with what had been normal previously. At one point, my father made a threat to my youngest sister. She never clearly stated what the threat included, but it was crystal clear that not everyone was happy with the direction things were moving. My father and stepmother were so used to having everything in their favor and now it appeared they were losing control. They had been successful at keeping the girls and the boys separated, basically pitting us against each other.

But now, everything was different and that was proving to be too much for them. So, it was suggested by my brother Bob and sister Stephanie that I should sit down with my father and stepmother to attempt to iron things out. Being the oldest, the only practicing Christian, and the one who had grown closer to becoming unoffendable, I seemed like the obvious choice. I called my father and set up the meeting time. When I arrived, the first few minutes were filled with these words, "We cannot trust Stephanie anymore! We feel like we are on the outside looking in." These words were repeated over and over. Their tone was quite fearful, like they were in great trepidation as if they had lost something and didn't know how to get it back.

I said to them, "We all want to **belong**. There exists an innate feeling inside every person to **belong**. The desire never goes away, wanting to **belong**. It's surprising to me that all it took to strip you both of your **belonging** and to lose trust in Stephanie was to have (all) your children begin to talk."

We spent the next four and one-half hours talking about many things. Our conversation included the years of frustration that my brothers and I had felt, the constant separation of family, the downright awful comments and talking behind each other's backs. We attempted to bring everything into the light. At one point my stepmother said to me, "How were we supposed to know all these things?"

To which I replied, "Cindy, I cannot hold you accountable for what you don't know. But now you have opened the door by asking that question. From now on, you don't get to say those words anymore, 'I didn't know.' You have now played that card and you won't be able to use that excuse any longer."

When it was time for me to leave, my father said the weirdest thing to me as I was walking out, "I can't believe you guys didn't take me with you." My father was somehow angry and hurt that we didn't take him with us, we didn't invite him to the meeting when we decided to be a unified family. We knew that if we couldn't unite ourselves first, he would never be able to either. Besides, he hadn't been able to unite us all these years.

As I was driving home, I kept thinking, "Isn't it odd that the father of the family wanted the children to bring him into unity? I thought it was the dad's job to unite the family. I thought he always said we were never two families but always one. If we were one, why did he lose his **belonging**? Why were they suddenly on the outside looking in? How come Stephanie's parents could not trust her any longer? Why did he want his children to bring him to this unified place if that's where we always were?"

I spent some time debriefing with my siblings. I told them that there had barely been an ounce of repentance on the part of either parent. In fact, they both felt like they were mostly right. Because of their blindness to the whole situation, I didn't think that anything good would come of it. Again, my siblings asked me to make a visit. I agreed to their second request and made the necessary arrangements to visit my father and stepmother the following week. Upon arriving, both my father and stepmother were hesitant and reserved. I explained to them that the work to repair the damage to this family was going to be monumental. If they were going to help, they would have to take responsibility for the things that they had done and learn to lead this family back to unity. Again, they pushed back and said, "We don't feel that we have done much wrong, if anything at all."

I replied, "That is exactly why I am here for the second time in two weeks. You two made the choice to bring this family forward. You never asked anyone else for their opinion. There has been constant unrest for more than three decades because you have never, for even a single moment, attempted to blend us. Your children have laid a foundation for family unity, basically we are serving it up on a silver platter for you both. With so much hanging in the balance are you now going to dig your heels in even further? Do I understand the circumstances correctly?"

At this, they both decided that they did not like the way I framed the situation and decided that all we had to do was learn to treat each other better. I exclaimed, "WOW! Is that all we must do? We just need to treat each other better?" I further stated, "Everyone in this family has contributed to the circumstances we are currently sitting in. Every one of us will have to take their share of responsibility. If you were part of the problem, then you must be part of the solution. As the parents, you set the example. You don't get to blame everyone else. That's not how this works. Did we learn our bad behaviors from you? Or did you learn them from us and then decide to implement them into your parenting skills? Everyone else has already begun taking responsibility for their part. Now it's up to you both to do yours."

They still didn't like how they were made to feel responsible as the parents. So, I told them to do whatever they thought was necessary to begin to lay a proper foundation for reconciliation. But I made it very clear when I said, "There are many people involved in this tragedy. Whatever you decide to call our situation and however you decide to handle taking your part of it, please make sure your plan blankets every person. If your umbrella does not cover all the people involved, you will never move this ship forward. Just make it simple for yourself and apologize to everyone and then tell them you will make every effort to never repeat the wrongs that have been perpetrated." They both agreed to consider my words and then proceed with their plan of action. Unfortunately, the following week, the world shut down because of the pandemic known as COVID-19. We were plagued like so many other families for the next two years. My ***belonging*** would have to wait.

Almost

James 4:17 (NIV), "If anyone, then, knows the good they ought to do and doesn't do it, it is sin for them."

In 2021, with the effects of COVID-19 now under control and people able to mingle freely, many members of my family were waiting for my father to assert his leadership and bring the family together for the very first time. Remember, his children had pretty much teed up all the foundational work for him. If he would display a bit of humility and an ounce of regret, we would be on our way. Finally, we might secure what we had waited so very long for, ***belonging***. That is when things began to slowly unravel.

It started with another visit to his house. I am part of a Tuesday morning Bible study called DIG (Digging into God). One of our members was still recovering from some outpatient surgery. I suggested to Joe that if he was up to it, we would come to his house for the Bible study instead of our usual meeting place. This way, he did not have to travel. Joe said that would be great. So, I asked Joe for his address. As it turned out, Joe lives 5 houses down the street from my father. Knowing that I would be in the area, I reached out to my father and asked if I could come over after the study. He and his wife said, "Yes, please do." Every time I entered my father's presence for the previous 25 plus years, he would slander both of my brothers in the opening conversation. When I say every time, I am not exaggerating. That day was no different.

The first thing he said to me was, "Your brother James is never going to get his life in order, if he doesn't figure it out soon, I'll be done with him. Your brother Bob is still drunk texting me. When will he learn?"

"Good morning dad," I replied. We spoke about nothing important for a few minutes and then he offered me a coffee. He reminded me that he had to leave soon because he had a doctor appointment.

Then, out of the blue my father said, "Jeff, I don't like you. I used to like you. There was a time when we had good times together, but not anymore. I don't like who you are. I don't like how you live. I don't like what you believe. I just don't like you!" This might bring a flood of emotion for most people, but this was not the first time I had heard this from my father.

When he finished his rant, I excused myself so he could get to his doctor appointment. Four days later, I was speaking to my brother Bob on the phone. During the conversation I let him know that I had stopped by our father's house a few days earlier. He asked how it went. I stated, "It wasn't the best and it wasn't the worst."

To which he replied, "You know, the last few times I have texted dad, it almost seemed like we were really making some progress. It's like he is really trying to make this work."

I questioned, "Really?"

My brother Bob stated, "Yes, he and I have carried on a few back-and-forth conversations. It appears to me that we may be moving in the right direction."

To that I said, "I am surprised that he would be awake that late at night."

Bob asked, "What do you mean late at night?" To which I stated, "Dad told me you were drunk texting him again and he seemed frustrated by it." Bob was obviously hurt and angry.

He asked, "Why would he dirty something up that was pure and innocent?" I stated, "Remind yourself of who you are talking about."

I wanted to talk to my father about this incident. It seemed to me that nothing had changed. He was still demonstrating the same awful behavior of vilifying his children. I thought, if we spoke about it, maybe he would show a bit of repentance. This would be a sign that we could move forward because some growth had taken place. When I entered his house, my stepmother, my father, and I each sat in the exact same places we had been in my previous visit. But this time, my father came at me aggressively screaming accusations. He shouted, "I cannot believe you told your brother I told you he was drunk texting me."

I responded, "Dad, it didn't happen in the way you think it did. But it doesn't take away the fact that you said it. It's interesting to me that you left out some important parts. Like, you were conversing and exchanging pleasantries. You were communicating in the morning hours, instead of the ugly picture that you painted of him texting you on the way home from the bar at night."

My father retorted, "I cannot believe you would do this to me."

I replied, "Dad, I didn't do anything. You did this to yourself. You robbed a liquor store. Instead of repenting and asking for forgiveness, you are just angry that someone turned you in. Your integrity is in question. Your character is damaged. And someone else is always at fault." That's when things got super weird, even for my father.

Now my father asked, "Why did you tell people that I said I didn't like you?"

To which I replied, "Isn't that exactly what you said? Even with our past, I can't believe that you think it is either appropriate or acceptable behavior to say such things."

At this point, my stepmother realized that this was really, unusually ugly, and she tried to put a stop to it. She screamed, "Your father never said that!"

I responded, "We were all sitting here, and we all heard the same thing. We also know it wasn't the first time it was stated. Why do you want to pretend it didn't happen?"

Again, she shouted, "He didn't say it!"

Then my father piped in, "Cindy, don't tell me what I didn't say! I know what I said! I told him I didn't like him. The first time I meant it but this time I didn't mean it."

At this point, I felt it was necessary to reel-in the situation so we can all get a hold of what we are doing and where we are in the circumstance. So, I question my dad, "Let me make sure I understand our current circumstances. You say that you don't like me. I am visiting your house and we only have 30 minutes to be together because you have a doctor appointment. The smartest thing you can think to say, in our time together, is that you don't like your son. After all the years of conflict, all the pain, all the hurt, all the drama, always blaming other people, it's never your fault, the best thing you can say is that you don't like your son. Your wife sees how ugly the situation is and she tries to put a stop to it. But your pride steps in and tells her you know exactly what you said. Additionally, there is some sort of *context* that determines when you mean, 'I don't like you,' and other times the *context* determines that you don't mean it. But the only person who knows the *context* is you. Now I am the bad guy here? I somehow, dishonestly, let people know that you said you didn't like your son. Do I understand the situation correctly?"

At this my father remained silent. So, I add, "Dad, I find it interesting that you would say these ugly words to me for no apparent reason. I also find it interesting that you never take responsibility for your actions, always blaming others, always painting yourself as the victim. But what really fascinates me is the fact that neither you, nor your wife, ever thinks it would be appropriate to apologize. To say, I can't believe I said something so terrible. Please forgive me, I was so wrong. I am so sorry. I love you son and I want us to be in a better place. Dad, do you know why apologizing never comes to your mind? Because you have never done it. Ever, in your life. Ever!"

At this my father did what he normally does when he has nowhere to run or hide. He doubles down. He said emphatically, "Yeah, so!"

Belonging is something that I believe a father should provide to his son, but in mine and my brother's case, it waits.

Acceptance

Romans 15:5-7 (NIV), "May the God who gives endurance and encouragement give you the same attitude of mind toward each other that Christ Jesus had, so that with one mind and one voice you may glorify the God and Father of our Lord Jesus Christ. Accept one another, then, just as Christ accepted you, in order to bring praise to God."

For the first time in a long time, one of my sisters was planning to come to my house for our family Christmas gathering. It has been nearly 20 years since my father, stepmother, and both sisters had attended regularly. However, only Lindsay could come this year because Stephanie lived in Maryland. Of course, it goes without saying, my father and stepmother would not be attending because of our family circumstances. I had hosted Christmas ever since my eldest son Matthew was born, 26 years. My mother has always attended this gathering, but this particular year she decided she was not going to come. She and I spoke on the phone about her decision to miss the family Christmas Party. My mother disclosed that she was extremely unhappy that my sister, not her daughter, would be attending. My mother did not want anyone from my father's family to interfere with her family gatherings, especially at Christmas.

I said, "Mom, I think you should be there. Everyone is going to miss you. Everyone is going to wonder why you did not come. What should I tell them?"

My mom stated, "Tell them I am sick, and don't feel good. But truthfully, I just don't want to share my holiday with them."

I reminded my mother, "Divorce is a very strange entity. It's always lurking, waiting for someone to devour. Just when you think it's gone, that you somehow put it behind you, it surfaces all over again."

My mom replied, "I can't do it. I can't share space with them. I am not going to come."

I exclaimed, "Mom, 46 years ago you made the decision, along with my father, to get a divorce. Neither of you consulted me or my brothers about what we wanted, how we felt, or if there was another choice in the matter. You both did what you wanted at the time. Neither of you could know what would happen in the years to come. But this moment in front of you is a direct consequence of *your* decision. Not mine! Yours! I can't fix it for you. You will have to do that all by yourself. This is *my* house, and these girls are *my* sisters, and there will be no division in *my* house."

At this, my mother was a bit startled, but she decided to attend. When she arrived, it was a little awkward, but we muddled through it and managed to enjoy the night. One of the other gross things about divorce is the effect it can have on any innocent person caught in its snare. My mother and I went through this whole uncomfortable episode for no reason. It turned out that my niece was not feeling well, so my sister never ended up coming that night. Our family was hindered again by the ugliness of divorce even though nothing had occurred. It did however reveal that acceptance was not at the ready.

Some months later, I approached my mother again about what had occurred at our Christmas gathering. At first, my mother did not want to talk about it. In fact, she refused. However, I told her that she was owed an apology. Again, she said stubbornly, "I don't want to hear it."

To which I replied, "Mom, why would you turn down an apology? I would think everyone would want to hear 'I am sorry' from anyone who wronged them? Why are you acting so brazen?"

My mom replied, "I can't and won't talk about it. It's done. Please leave it alone!"

I exclaimed, "Mom, I was wrong. I am sorry. Please forgive me. I love you! I tried to force you into something that you were not ready for. Forced acceptance is not acceptance. The result I was looking for was right, but the manner in which I went about it was wrong. My sisters are not your family, and I should have never violated our family time by inviting them. You deserve my apology because in forcing you, I was not loving you or respecting you." At this point, my mother finally let her guard down and we talked through the conflict. Since then, we have repaired our relationship.

These are the types of moments that continue to bring my family discomfort. I am sure there are many families experiencing the same ill-effects because of divorce. When families are plagued because there are people who cannot provide *belonging*, what usually ends up happening is the comparison game. Instead of addressing the issues at hand, most people spend their time comparing the egregiousness of their conflict so they can make themselves feel better. However, this does nothing to build or restore *belonging*, and only serves to create more bad behaviors.

Familiar

Proverbs 14:29 (NIV), "Whoever is patient has great understanding but one who is quick-tempered displays folly."

As my family's circumstances continued to linger, my brother James decided to ask our sister Stephanie some questions about inheritance. James asked these questions with curiosity, but based on our family's storied familiarity, he suspected that he already knew most of the answers. When our momentum to blend our family began to stall, and the decisions became more complex and more difficult to execute, James went looking for answers to our future. Stephanie was apparently quite surprised when she realized that James had hopes that our attempt to blend our family meant that we would all be equal in every sense of the word. One of the things we agreed upon in our original conversation, among all five siblings, was that no one person is more important than another. Every one of us has the same intrinsic value. If we weren't going to be equal, there would be no point in moving forward. This was our focus, or so we thought. Next, Stephanie decided to test the waters with me. She had already been displeased with James' question and his response, so she wanted to see if there was a common theme among us.

Stephanie approached me about her conversation with James. She decided to play off our experience of the previous Christmas where James hosted. James thought that catering the meal would be a great idea. But when he passed on the cost to everyone, most of the family were very unhappy. James was attempting to remove the inconvenience from their busy schedules. However, most of them could not see that James was attempting to do something nice. So, this was the root of Stephanie's penetrating question concerning what she had talked about with James previously regarding inheritance. I told Stephanie that I was not going to squabble over a little bit of money for a family dinner, especially since I could see what James had attempted to do.

At this, Stephanie stated, "I am glad you feel that way, because we must talk about inheritance. James feels like he should be included when our father dies. I cannot imagine why he would ever think that he would receive a portion of any inheritance?"

I responded, "Stephanie, I don't think you should compare a family dinner to an inheritance. They are vastly different." She wanted to know why James was so upset by her indifferent attitude. I said to Stephanie, "Whether you realize it or not, James has had it worse than any of us. He was two years old when my mother and your father divorced. He doesn't own a memory of normal. He has never had the pleasure of being our father's favorite. He was always treated like a leper. When I was in my early 20's, there was a rumor floating through this family that James was not our father's son. No one put that rumor to rest. Everyone let it linger. James was left to wonder, and maybe he still does. James has never had our father's complete, uninterrupted, attention except for a brief stint for a couple of months while he was married to his second wife. I remember James's countenance changed abruptly for the better when he finally tasted *belonging* from our father. He was so happy. But as quickly as ***belonging*** was given to him, it was also stripped away just as quickly by our father. James has been the brunt of so many ugly moments. Hopefully now, Stephanie, you can understand why he is searching for ***belonging***."

At this, Stephanie changed course. She began to complain that James, Bob, and myself had a bond that we were never going to let her be a part of. I replied, "It's one of the greatest tragedies in the world, divorce. There are many ills in the world but none so silently deadly as divorce. It kills more than half the families in the world. It's unnatural, and never loosens its grip, constantly lingering in the lives of those caught in it. Even the people who have a foreknowledge of the ills of divorce cannot prepare themselves for what awaits. Your children will never hear or experience what ours did. Nor will you ever know what my experience has been like. I don't hold that against you. It's not your fault. You stated that you wanted to break into the bond that I share with Bob and James and that you needed assurance? We all want assurance, it's only natural. Some of the threads of the bond I share with Bob and James formed by simply growing up in the same house. Some of the threads formed because our parents walked us into something called divorce. Their choices stole our unity and sent us on a journey that can't be undone. As you might imagine, much of it was not good. So, who do you hold onto when you don't have stability? Your siblings! Some of those threads formed when our father and your mother decided they wanted a family of their own. The only problem was they did not know what they would face and did not know how to blend us."

I continued, "So, I ask again, who do you hold onto when you don't have stability? Your sibling(s). This bond has formed over a number of years and through a lifetime of ills. The fact that we share a bond of that nature is not our fault and it's not your fault. It became necessary when there was nothing else. Could someone else be included in this bond? Maybe, possibly, probably. Understanding why the bond was birthed in the first place would be helpful. But that would require someone to have perspective. Many don't. That bond is similar to a family; a deep trust that you are as equal as all the other parts. Believing without a doubt that the bond continues to grow (for that is the very nature of a bond) through a constant nurturing and fighting to protect that unity all the while trusting that all the other parts are doing the same. This provides a deep **belonging** that everyone craves. Divorce does not provide that. Divorce means split, broken, fragmented, and separate. Having an 'un-blended or fragmented' family does not provide that either. In fact, both divorce and un-blended are similar unless *intentional* blending occurs. Any attempt to procure unity from something that is broken requires every person to be willing to exert greater attention to that type of bond if it is to form. There must be a trust built, developed over time, that all are one and all have the same intrinsic value. Stephanie, we have never done this. It's not your fault and it's not mine. I won't even blame the people whose choices brought us to this place, that would mean they knew what awaited them. They did not."

Hearing this, Stephanie said that she would need some time to think about everything. She ended up sitting in silence for 30 days. Perhaps she wanted to make sure she had all the right words to share with us when she was ready. When she emerged, there was little doubt that something was different. Suddenly the words that my brother James shared with our sisters a couple of years previously proved to be prophetic. The difficulty of our family circumstances would make any decision-making almost impossible. Stephanie stated she was growing in dislike because of both the direction and ultimately the destination that our conversations were heading. She postured that she and Lindsey were the only ones who were going to receive any inheritance. She said her parents had not only stated it verbally but had also written it in legal documentation. When Stephanie held this position for more than a week, she and I had a conversation about unity and doing the right thing despite a poor choice our parents may have made. We talked about what we all had agreed upon, that no one would be left behind, that everyone has equal standing.

Upon hearing this, Stephanie decided to place the responsibility on her parents. She said, "Why am I being held responsible for choices that I never made?"

I replied, "Stephanie, these are the impossible choices that innocent people are thrust into when grown adults do not think things through before making life changing choices that affect other people." I believe it was in that moment that Stephanie truly succumbed to the realization that there was no way out. We were either going to push forward with continuously difficult, almost impossible choices, or she would have to stick to her guns and hold her position.

I asked Stephanie, "When you leave this planet, are you willing to award one of your daughters whatever you have amassed and leave nothing to your other daughter?"

She said, "Of course not! I would never do such a thing. That would be horrible. I have more sense than that!"

So, I asked, "If that is true, then why are you so willing to help your parents do the same thing to James, Bob, and myself." Our conversation abruptly ended with that question.

At one point, a few days after this conversation, Stephanie stated emphatically, "I will not allow you to have the final F.U. on my father."

In our final exchange, I said, "What hurts most about this is that you have shared too much Stephanie. You have tasted drops in the ocean your brothers have been made to swim in. You made it known that you disliked the taste. Now imagine swallowing gallons of that distaste over the years. I don't wish it on anyone. I won't hold it against you as I love you, it's not your fault. You asked me why you should be held accountable for choices you did not make. I want the same afforded to me. Nonetheless, where there is not unity and fairness afforded to all, choices are impossible. James was right when he said to you that night in Troy that he felt sorry for you. I should have never let you enter that space. Just as your parents did not know the challenges that awaited them because of the choices they made all those years ago, you could not have known either. Impossible is what awaited you. It was unfair. But that is the place we all find ourselves living now; the impossible."

Sadly, Lindsey and I never spoke about this topic. Lindsey is never one to introduce conflict, she runs from it because she doesn't like to talk about difficult subjects. She always held onto her parent's position more than the greater sum of our family. She did this because that is all she knows, that's how she and Stephanie were raised. Neither of them has the perspective to see beyond their normal family unit. To do anything else would be almost impossible for her as she would have to fight off the *familiar*. Because of this, she has never wanted to make a stand for unity. Her loyalty, much like Stephanie, my stepmother, and my father to their family tribe, is strong. But their desire for truth has never been seen, felt, or heard. A desire for truth would include my brothers and I. That would mean we **belonged**. Unfortunately, that has never been on the table for us.

Once again, my brothers and our families were back where we started. The place my brothers and I have lived for more than four decades, where our children have lived their whole lives. We are on the outside staring in. All we wanted was to **belong** to our family. My brother James was reluctant from the start. He didn't want to get hurt once again. But still, I convinced him we should walk ahead in faith. I have since apologized to James for convincing him to trust me. Always with my father we are invited to *stare* at the circle but never are we invited *into* the circle to be *part* of the circle. We are free to make visits when it's picture time if we play by the rules. But dad and his household never let you forget that you are nothing more than a guest.

Some might wonder why it appears that an inheritance would keep a family apart? The fact is that inheritance did not keep my family apart. Inheritance was just another roadblock in a series of roadblocks that my family has yet to overcome to find unity and **belonging**. This dichotomy only serves to prove that **belonging** is not automatically given, regardless of the family dynamic, and those caught in the arms of divorce continue to smell its ugly stench. Inheritance is most certainly not in the mind of the blended-family parent when they re-marry because they are never looking that far down the road. Neither is it in the mind of the child, that is, until you don't know if you **belong**. Under what circumstances would a parent remove their children's rights as their heir? Why would someone willingly exclude one or more of their children? Why wouldn't they exclude them all? Why would someone cause division with their last request and final legacy?

These are exactly the questions Stephanie pondered about her own children and could easily decide in their favor. I suspect *most* parents are of the same opinion. I know it couldn't have been easy for Stephanie to help facilitate our father and her mother's desire to remove that right from my brothers and me. I don't know if she realizes it or not, but in making that choice, she decided that her husband had more of a right than mine or my brother's wives, and she decided her children had more of a right than mine or my brother's children.

The hope to **belong** is set aside once again. Will we ever find **belonging** here? The jury is still out. But consider this, how is it possible for any of us to seek justice, another offering of **belonging**, for those outside our own families if we neglect to seek justice for those within our families?

> *Micah 6:8 (NIV), "He has shown you, O mortal, what is good. And what does the Lord require of you? To act justly and to love mercy and to walk humbly with your God."*

Did *familiar* win? Maybe because we are so accustomed to being separate, Stephanie returned to what was *familiar* to her. Perhaps Stephanie felt like she had no good choice? This is what most of us do when change becomes too costly. Most of us self-protect. Maybe Stephanie thought it best for her and her family to pursue their own **belonging**, and she wanted me and my brothers to do the same?

These are just a few of the impossible choices that await children of divorce. Perhaps our separation in this generation paves the way for a lesser chance of leaving behind a curse for the next generation? This is exactly why we receive only the beginning of our understanding and experience of our **belonging** from our family. Because, only in Christ does **belonging** fully mature, grow, and strengthen.

> *Galatians 3:24-29 (NIV), "So the law was our guardian until Christ came that we might be justified by faith. Now that this faith has come, we are no longer under a guardian. So in Christ Jesus you are all children of God through faith, for all of you who were baptized into Christ have clothed yourselves with Christ. There is neither Jew nor Gentile, neither slave nor free, nor is there male and female, for you are all one in Christ Jesus. If you **belong** to Christ then you are Abraham's seed, and heirs according to the promise."*

Family is important, but if your identity is caught up more in a temporal family identity than in being a child of God, your priorities are off. Only in Christ can you find true **belonging**. In Christ, you never have to earn the rights and privileges bestowed upon you as an adopted child, and you never have to worry that your **belonging** will be taken away. You never have to vex about being good enough. You never have to question your worth. You don't have to worry if justice will prevail. When you **belong** to Christ, you have the same intrinsic value as every other person. Your ***belonging*** is seated in you and becomes a part of you.

Deleted

2 Corinthians 3:14 (NIV), "But their minds were made dull, for to this day the same veil remains when the old covenant is read. It has not been removed, because only in Christ is it taken away."

The following story is my brother Bobs memory of how our hope of ***belonging*** will always remain a mystery. Generational curses in the Bible do not refer to witchcraft and voodoo. Generational curses refer to the behaviors, habits, and customs of the previous generation that were never altered or changed, and thus passed down. Because of our rather odd difference in age, we watched as our sisters carried on the tradition of leaving my brothers and I out of our family. Should we try to fight, yet another generation of people, just to have a place established on shifting sand? How long will our voices be unheard? For now, our ***belonging*** will have to wait, once again.

{Bob's story}

The relationship with our sisters, Stephanie, and Lindsey, began to fracture and fade. There were less conversations, phone calls, etc. What was once a daily ritual, reaching out to each other, had now become a chore. It was obvious to everyone that something had changed. Jeff, James, and I took a trip to Cleveland for the weekend. When we returned, our sisters started commenting negatively. They felt slighted that they were not invited. What's ironic is the fact that we were originally headed to Stephanie's house in Bethesda, Maryland for a long weekend, until she became concerned about COVID. Then she asked us not to come. So, instead, we went to Cleveland. That did not stop the girls from questioning and complaining to us.

I explained, "Jeff was struggling, still missing his son deeply and just needed to talk. Cleveland (middle of December, freezing cold) was just an excuse to drive in the car and let Jeff talk… our job was to listen." Because of the age difference and different stations in life.... my brothers and I don't require a babysitter or someone to cover for dance lessons, practice, etc., our kids are grown. We, the boys, can just head out without much planning or notice. Our sisters have schedules, young families… they are busy as young parents always are. I thought driving to Cleveland for a couple of nights was no big deal. The Cleveland trip was just the example my sister's needed to prove their theory/opinion and justify their feelings that we were not sharing equally.

Shortly after our trip to Cleveland, my father reached out to me. He wanted to meet and discuss some things. My father and I have completed this exercise many times, but nothing ever changes. Regardless, I agreed to meet him at a restaurant centrally located between both of our homes. As usual, he is very friendly with the waitress. It's not odd or rare as my father is well liked by everyone, except for the family he left behind. That disparity always leads to an odd disconnect between mutual acquaintances my brothers and I share with our father (on occasion), but that is a discussion for another day.

Tonight, I have a bigger mission, so I let all the "BS" fall to the side. I have always attempted to help my father mend the connection between my brothers and our families. I have always been jovial, emotional (to tears sometimes) and pleaded with him to change. He was the best man at my wedding, and of course the person I idolized most.

Tonight, I am calloused, I will not be his friend. I am here to defend my daughters, nieces, and nephews. No longer am I worried about myself, my brothers, or our spouses. It's been too long, our father… my father…the man I knew, loved, respected, and idolized died a long time ago. He is here to defend his daughters, their families and try to impress his wishes on me. He would like nothing more than to have everyone hug and move on…. I tell him again… "An apology is necessary and owed, at a minimum. Some of these kids, my nieces and nephews, your grandchildren, are now young adults. They have spent their entire life without their grandfather. At the very least you owe them an apology."

My father replies, "It wasn't always easy." Then he shared the same lines he always does. He finishes with, "Families are busy… mine, yours, our friends, our neighbors… all of them."

I questioned loudly, "BUSY? For the last 25-plus years you've been busy?" I got angry. My skin began to crawl. I knew he was wasting my time.

Once he knew I wasn't going to give in to his quick fix and forget the last 25-plus years… he became very business-like.

Reconciliation was out the window. My father could tell I was tense and wanted to end the "meeting" as quickly as possible. I wanted to leave him with something he could ponder. I began to talk about my sister Stephanie's family. I wanted him to know that Stephanie and her husband Jake had felt like they and their children were forgotten, less than, second best, not a priority. Stephanie's youngest was about to have her first birthday party and it was known that my father wasn't sure he could attend. Stephanie was hurt and confused. She and I had discussed my father not attending multiple times. My father and I discussed it. He used these ridiculous excuses; they live far away… I don't like to fly… driving that distance is not my idea of a good time.

In the most direct way possible, I exclaimed these statements to my father, "Why must you travel and share time with Stephanie, her husband, and their kids? Why? Because it's necessary. It's necessary to create a bond with your grandchildren and make memories they will never forget. IT'S NECESSARY! Do not do to those babies (Steph's daughters were only three and nearly one at the time) what you have done to Jeff, James, myself, our spouses, and our children. It's too late for all of us. Learn from your mistakes and do the right thing for those babies. Spend the time, make the trip, send the text, write the letter, send the card, pick up the phone, and for God's sake attend your granddaughter's first birthday party. Your daughter is praying you'll be there." We parted ways. I knew this was quite possibly the last time I'd see my father.

Sometime in the months following my meeting with my father, Stephanie reached out to me. She was looking for reassurance regarding any/all future inheritance should our father pass away. I knew she broached the subject with my brother James, and she knew that I had already spoken to both my brothers. Therefore, I knew both of my brothers' opinions (positions) on the subject. Among my brothers, I was probably the closest to Stephanie, and naively believed she would consider all parties when tasked with the responsibility of inheritance. I said to her, "No worries, Stephanie, as the executor you have the power to correct the mistake." I fully believed she would consider my brothers and I, our families, etc., as equal parts. She and I entered a long-drawn-out conversation.

She stated, "I don't feel like we (the five siblings) have the "bond" we should, and we never will. Besides, I have a legal responsibility to follow my parent's direction." Our conversation went on for hours.

I finally said, "If you don't view us as equals then do the right thing and pass any/all proceeds down to our children (her parent's grandchildren). These kids have suffered enough. Any proceeds could help them pay for college, or assist with a down payment on a house, or whatever… at least one good thing could come from their grandfather."

At that point, Stephanie began to tell me that she didn't see our relationship moving forward. I reminded her that our father had begun to treat her and her family similar to the way he had treated my brothers and our families. I reminded her that her own daughters had been treated as less than and not a priority. In the last year, Stephanie and I had shared our pain and had deep conversations regarding our father. We discussed the pain our nieces and nephews had lived through their entire lives because their grandfather had little or zero interest in spending or investing time to get to know them (most were in their early 20's by now). I said, "Stephanie, you must understand that our father has never come for these kids. Never attended a game, never attended a choir concert, never attended a graduation from kindergarten or high school. He has done the same to me, my brothers, and our spouses."

After hearing this, Stephanie said something I will never forget. She stated, "He might not have come for you or any of them, but he came for me." This meant that our father attended her daughter's first birthday celebration. I sat in my car, understanding at that moment she had made her decision. She was severing the relationship with my brothers and our families. The line of separation was clear. The attempt to create real change was over, we were never family, nor will we ever be. It was all a façade. Stephanie was willing to forsake everyone as long as she and her family were cared for. With that, Stephanie ended our conversation in this way, "I wish you the best, but I no longer see any future in a relationship with you." When things begin to get tough, *familiar* tends to rear its ugly head, and we are always certain to find out if we **belong** or if we do not **belong**.

Fragile

Isaiah 64:6 (NIV), "All of us have become like one who is unclean, and all our righteous acts are like filthy rags; we all shrivel up like a leaf, and like the wind our sins sweep us away."

The brokenness of our family surfaced, and we were frozen yet again. Difficult conversations continue to be impossible to overcome. Everyone returns to the side from which they feel comfortable. Division wins out over unity. This is the cycle from which my unblended family cannot escape. Considering all the turmoil that has taken place, I shared some words in an email to my father with hopes that maybe one day we will be united. This is how it read:

Dad,

Clarity is not always provided to us no matter how hard we try to understand. Over the years I have tried many times to explain the circumstances of our plight, but it never seemed to land. Perspective is not something you can give away. People must earn it through their own experience.

I have always held out hope that one day we could work things out. That hope was heightened when "all" your children started talking about unity and family and doing it right. I remember sitting in your living room just before COVID hit and hoping we were finally on our way to reconciliation. I remember the words you and Cindy stated repeatedly, "We cannot trust Stephanie anymore" and "We feel like we're on the outside looking in." Your tone was fearful, like you were in great trepidation, as if you had lost something and didn't know how to get it back. We all want to belong. It's an innate desire that never goes away, wanting to belong. That day, it was like your belonging was taken from you. Surprisingly, all it took to strip you of both your belonging and trust in your daughter Stephanie was to have "all" your children begin to talk.

If at some point over the years I could have painted a picture that properly demonstrated that very experience, feeling like being on the outside looking in, perhaps we might be in a different place today. However, I was never able to provide a clear enough picture for you. I am not certain how long you both felt that way, a few days, or a few weeks, or possibly even a few months? What I would like you to know is that your sons have lived in that space for more than four decades. Your own experience, although brief, might provide clues to how your sons felt. All we wanted and needed was to know that we belonged. Sure, sometimes you would mouth the words, but actions rarely followed. If they did, they never lasted. It's easy to say, and hard to display. Unfortunately, we didn't receive that from you.

I have spent much of my life trying to understand the ills of divorce and the attempt people make to blend families. I did it because you wouldn't or couldn't hear me whenever I came to you for answers. You never stopped to listen. You never sought to understand. You never changed directions. You never made any adjustments. You just kept going down the same path. I needed to understand why this was happening and why I could not find belonging.

Every problem has a starting point and if we trace it back long enough, we can find its origin. I don't resent you dad for our circumstances. You complicated your life and like most people you did the best you could. Neither you nor Cindy could have seen or even thought about all the difficulties you would face. That does not make you a bad person. Most people never want to get to the root, or the truth, of the problem because it would cause them to have to move from their position and see things from a different vantage point. We all knew reconciliation would be difficult, but we set out to accomplish it anyway. After all, we were never a blended family, fragmented maybe, but not blended. Maybe you were so consumed with trying to figure out how to get your own belonging back that you missed the bigger catch? With closed hands you cannot receive new blessings.

Clarity? In the end dad, we do have something in common after all. That short season when you felt like you were on the outside looking in and when you couldn't trust Stephanie anymore will always provide the answer to why our struggles never ended. All it took for you to lose your belonging was for "all" your children to begin to talk. Now think about how easy it was to steal and how fragile it was in your hands. Then ask yourself, "If we were so blended and so close as a family, how could I feel this way?" Then think about how it must have felt for three boys cast on the outside looking in, by choices they did not make, by parents who didn't know how to navigate the most challenging of circumstances. Because, in the end, they never belonged!

Your son,

Jeff

Why do families hurt each other? Why can't families solve the conflict that threatens their unity? Are we, as a society, spending more time placing band-aids on bullet holes instead of concentrating on fixing the root of our problems? The circumstances in my family are not that uncommon. What is so unnerving is that we appear to be headed to greater separation while unity seems more distant. Will my family ever figure it out? That question remains unlikely to be answered.

Peace

John 16:33 (NIV), "I have told you these things, so that in me you may have peace. In this world you will have trouble. But take heart! I have overcome the world."

Love is a road that's easier to preach about than walk down. When the sweet sentiments and good intentions of love meet the reality of stressful life and so many needy people, sometimes loving your neighbor doesn't seem so practical. Still, Jesus calls us to love with our lives.

My family is still trapped by decades of brokenness and dysfunction that has never been dealt with. We have graduated only to a greater awareness that we are more broken than we had ever known. It's hard enough to solve the problems that a nuclear family may face, but starting from brokenness, merging families, and then never putting in the time or the effort to repair what is broken just makes everything more complicated. Some members of my family are still blind, possibly unwilling to face the mountains ahead. Some are still attempting to place band-aids on our bullet holes thinking this time it will work. Some can't understand why others won't just take the crumbs that are offered and be happy. Others have screamed they will never again submit themselves to the depth of the all too familiar, painful, reality of hoping for reconciliation and watching it vanish before their eyes.

Only when the concerns move beyond the individual and to the greater good of the collective, will anything begin to change and ***belonging*** appear. Until every person has the same intrinsic value we may never find ***belonging*** and unity. When human knowledge continues to supersede Divine Wisdom, brokenness remains, and ***belonging*** elusive. What should we expect? What should any of us expect, especially when you start from a place that God never intended for us to travail, and then never invite Him to help us out of the darkness. Only in the Kingdom of God does every person find intrinsic value, equality, and ***belonging*** at the foot of the cross.

I have God's peace amid my family's chaos. I trust and pray that God will redeem my whole family the way He has redeemed me, and that ***belonging*** will be restored.

Psalm 107:2-3 (NIV), "Let the redeemed of the Lord tell their story—those he redeemed from the hand of the foe, those he gathered from the lands, from east and west, from north and south."

-Lessons Learned-

Most every person you meet throughout your entire life will at some point do, or say, something that is unkind and disrespectful. This includes your family members. Those people didn't wake up on a given day and think, "Today is so and so's bad day because I deemed it. Today is the day that I am going to harm them." When the people in our lives hurt us, they usually don't do so with intent. They simply give you the best they have in the moment. Hence, we hurt each other all the time. Conversely, if others are walking around inadvertently hurting us, then the opposite is also true. That means we are inadvertently hurting other people as well. Knowing this, we must take greater care with our words and our actions as they can have lasting effects. There are 12 words that should always be at the ready; *I was wrong; I am sorry; please forgive me; I love you!* If these words are spoken in the quick, many of our problems can be evaded. If your life is complicated because of divorce, it might be wise to consider everyone's views on the circumstances, not just your own. If you only consider your own circumstances, you unconsciously remove the ***belonging*** of those around you.

Love is the craving of the human heart to belong in the sacredness of trust and a relationship! (Author Unknown)

6

Emerging from Darkness

Throughout my childhood and for much of my adult life I did not know where I ***belonged*** or who I ***belonged*** to because I didn't know who I was. My identity was wrapped up in many things, my vocation, my experiences, and even my feelings. Different seasons of life brought different identities, and nothing sustained, nothing fulfilled, *nothing* grounded me. I was a friend of the world and it had me caught up living in "destination-bound thinking." Destination-bound thinking is lacking contentment in the "now" and believing that it will appear when you arrive at the next goal or stop. Having direction is better than having a goal. A better way to live is to practice "direction-bound thinking." Practicing direction-bound thinking provides the fortitude and strength of mind and body that can produce contentment in all circumstances. People who exert more energy concentrating on the destination often fail to enjoy the journey.

I always thought there was a place waiting for my arrival and when I finally got there, my life would be all I hoped it could be.

When I earn enough….. then.

When I accumulate enough….. then.

When I find the right….. then.

When I drive the right car….. then.

When I get the big house….. then.

The world always promises, but the world never delivers. It continually sucks you into thinking, now, I will be happy. But happiness is fleeting, it must be renewed over and over again. I was caught in the snare of this never-ending cycle. If you knew me back then, you could see evidence that my identity was found in either my performance, my possessions, or my popularity. Sometimes, you might even see confirmation of all three at the same time. These are, by the way, the exact three ways that Satan tempts us all. Coincidence? I think not! I was like a wave in an ocean being tossed around by the wind. What is more, I could not find my *belonging*.

1 John 2:15 (NIV), "Do not love the world or anything in the world. If anyone loves the world, love for the Father is not in them."

The most important thing about us—what defines our life and destiny—is often hidden from the view of others. It cannot be seen or praised by those around us. If we live for the affirmation of others, we are unlikely to give much attention to our foundations. The world celebrates the grandeur of the house, but the Lord alone knows the quality of its foundation.

For us to grow in the Lord, there must be a continual, personal surrender and discovery that God is bigger than you or I could ever imagine. To say that God is the Creator of all things may elicit some provocation of His grandeur. But to believe through revelation that the more you know of God, the more you realize that what you don't know becomes profound. Basically, we can never gain ground on God. As He reveals Himself to us, we marvel at our smallness. I remember when this concept started to become real to me. The Divine Nature of God is that of love. God has many things to show us, and many places to take us, but He cannot impart anything to us if we are not willing to receive. When we finally succumb to His will, we realize that there will always be something new to learn. Along the way to surrender, identity, and *belonging* there are many steps. Each step creates something new in us. We begin to look more like Him and less like us, and our identity and *belonging* are undergirded. In the same way that we can have greater measures of the fruit of the Spirit (love, joy, peace, forbearance, kindness, goodness, faithfulness, gentleness, and self-control) as we walk with the Lord, we can have greater undergirding of our identity and *belonging*.

Once we are secured in our *belonging*, it becomes important for us to both demonstrate, and attempt to give away *belonging* to others as we continue to journey through life. One of the biggest hindrances in finding *belonging* comes from our culture's inability to provide *belonging* because so many of us don't know who we are. You cannot give what you do not have.

Our awakening in the Lord isn't meant to be kept to ourselves. It is meant to be shared. It becomes an undeniable certainty inside of us that cannot be faked. When we are stirred by the goodness of God, we begin to understand that our victory is first for us and then for those around us. We must tell people about Jesus and all He has done for us. Instead of being caught up in the negativity of the world, we encourage others with the truth of our testimony. Our light is always shining no matter how dark our circumstances.

The extent of people who can share in this way and provide *belonging* appears to be quite small. Most of us are in a constant battle with our thoughts. We have an identity that comes from a horizontal place or thing instead of vertically in Christ. We are either living in the past, caught in our own guilt and shame, or living in the "what if" future of fear of the unknown. When we have a false identity, our minds are distracted, and we don't know how to be in the present. If we don't know how to live in the present, we are unable to provide space for those who are standing right in front of us. One of the giftings God has given me is the ability to be *with* people in their most difficult and challenging seasons of life. To hold space for another person is one of the greatest gifts we can offer anyone. Giving another person a sense of *belonging* is vital.

Have you ever wondered why we are such a shallow culture? Think about this…We have people standing in front of us every day with the same desire that we have, they want to *belong*. Most of us don't know who we are, we are longing to *belong* and thus are unable to give *belonging* to the person in front of us. Our minds are caught in the past or the future and the person in front of us never feels like they were seen or heard. Over time we condition ourselves with this type of practiced shallowness. Before long, there are droves of people who feel invisible and run from place to place to find *belonging*, all the while thinking that its hopeless. Many an addict has experienced this type of reception, especially from those who claim to love them.

When your identity is in Christ and your *belonging* is well-founded, you can sit with any person and listen intently to what they say. You can listen to hear and not to respond. You are able to let every word wash over you, even if the person has a totally different religious, political, or worldview than yours. A person whose identity is in Christ, with a secured *belonging,* can listen to any person and know that there are sprinkles of truth littered throughout their words. *Belonging* allows us to absorb what is valuable and release what is not in any conversation with any person. What's more, a person is heard, and a feeling of hopelessness may be removed.

In many cases, our love is as absent as our ***belonging***. Many people are very forward with their affections. They tend to help people on their own terms. Instead of providing what a person needs, we mostly give them what we want them to have. I used to be a part of a men's Bible study. In this study group there were men from all ages and backgrounds, including a homeless man. Well after the group was established and the men got to know each other well, the homeless man was robbed. During the night, someone stole his backpack. The next day, emails were flying back and forth between the men of the group. The men were upset that Mike's backpack was stolen, and they had plans of buying Mike many pairs of pants, shirts, shoes, socks, underwear, etc. I intervened and asked, "Why are you trying to solve Mike's problems through your eyes and not his? Mike does not have a dresser or a closet. Where do you think he will store all these items? Ask him how best to help and then you will be providing for his needs."

Giving someone what you want them to have may be a good thing but is it the best thing. We must learn to meet people right where they are and sit with them in their circumstances. Being present in the moment, being with people is what this world needs more than anything else. This is the best way for us to offer ***belonging*** to those who have yet to find it.

Mostly, we give people what we want them to have, instead of meeting their needs, because meeting their needs requires us to have to get uncomfortable, to get our hands dirty. The comforts of this world, the walls that surround our version of the gospel, our lack of vertical identity, and our **"not"** ***belonging*** all prevent us from loving people and sharing the treasure we have found with them.

Performance

James 1:22-25 (NIV), "Do not merely listen to the word, and so deceive yourselves. Do what it says Anyone who listens to the word but does not do what it says is like someone who looks at his face in a mirror and, after looking at himself, goes away and immediately forgets what he looks like. But whoever looks intently into the perfect law that gives freedom, and continues in it—not forgetting what they have heard, but doing it—they will be blessed in what they do."

"As man's obedience increases, his actions decrease. When we first begin to follow the Lord, we are full of activity but quite short of obedience. But as we advance in spirituality our actions gradually diminish until we are filled with obedience. Many, however, do what they like and refuse to do what they dislike. They never ponder whether or not they are acting out of obedience. Hence many works are done out of self and not in obedience to God" (Watchman Nee, Spiritual Authority).

Early in my faith journey, like many newer Christians, I always found there were more than enough good deeds that needed attending to. As long as the deeds don't take too much of our time or energy, we are always more than happy to tackle them. And because I was an overachiever, I found more than my fair share to consume. One of the areas of service that caught my eye was youth soccer. My sons were playing soccer in our area's recreational league and the leaders were always asking for help. So, it seemed like a good fit. At first, I started out slow, only occupying my time in one part of the league. But as time went on, I began to take on more and more responsibility. I started donating my time and energy in multiple areas and even became a board member. Before I knew it, I was giving this organization every evening Monday through Friday and my entire weekend. My kids were with me for some of the time and that is what kept me believing it was the right thing to do.

My performance was of utmost importance to me. Privately, among the board members, there were milestones and records of service that we were always trying to achieve and beat. Before long, my service was for all the wrong reasons, and I found myself searching and craving once again for **belonging**. As each soccer season passed, my time with the Lord was decreasing. I grew hungrier and thirstier for what was not being fed to me on the soccer field or from the service that no longer provided my **belonging**. Then one day I stopped at the local coffee shop. Normally I would simply grab my coffee and go, but on this day, I decided to look around and see who or what was there. To my surprise, I saw four men reading the Bible. I knew I had to stop by their table and introduce myself. When I got there, I said,

"Gentlemen, I cannot tell you how refreshing it is that you are reading the Bible. I have not been in God's Word for some time now."

They surprised me again, but this time with their words when they said, "Join us!" I left the coffee shop that day with tears in my eyes. God hadn't left me, and I had renewed joy and a refreshed spirit.

I was blessed to have been a part of the Coffee Shop Bible Study for seven years. During that time, the men of the group shared their wisdom and showed me how a Christian man was supposed to conduct himself. I gained more experience in ministry and service as we walked together in Bible study, fellowship, and discipleship. Over the years, some of the men left the group but there were always new men who joined. The group went through cycles where there were many men and then there were few. Then came the first day that I arrived to find that no one else had dragged themselves out of bed for the 6 a.m. Bible study. I was angry and felt disrespected. Not a single phone call or text message came across my phone.

A few weeks later, it happened again. Same thing! Not a single phone call or text message came across my phone. This time, I decided that a conversation was needed. Once is an accident, but twice? I thought maybe something had changed in the other men's schedules which caused them to not show up. After much conversation, it was determined that some of the men thought it wasn't worth it to show up for only a few people. With renewed intentions, however, each man made a pledge to be in attendance. For the next several weeks the attendance was spotty. However, it wasn't long before the inevitable happened. I was the only man to arrive. And once again, the same thing happened, not a single phone call or text message came across my phone. I prayed to God and asked for direction. I knew it was time to leave the group and find a new one. This time, God brought me to the community of men who were part of my church. I was delighted to be welcomed into the Bible study group called DIG (Digging into God). Once again, God renewed my spirit, and my **belonging** was strengthened.

Possessions

Matthew 6:19-21 (NIV), "Do not store up for yourselves treasures on earth, where moths and vermin destroy, and where thieves break in and steal. But store up for yourselves treasures in heaven, where moths and vermin do not destroy, and where thieves do not break in and steal. For where your treasure is, there your heart will be also."

For all my life, I have been enthralled with earthly treasures. I was consumed with how I can get more earthly treasures. Subsequently, I have always asked the question, "When will I find the earthly treasure that will provide more than a short supply of gratification and contentment?" In my case, and I suspect like many others, the day we meet Jesus our desire to hold onto earthly treasures begins to wane. Unfortunately, for those of us who live in the United States, there is a never-ending supply of shiny and new earthly treasures being thrown at us virtually every minute of the day. This compulsion still has its hooks in me to some degree. But my relationship with Jesus has shown me that our relationships are more important than any "thing" we might possess.

I remember when the pursuit of money was still my top priority. In my previous life (before Jesus), I was often away from the house for more than 250 days a year for work. As much as I didn't like being away from home, I wanted the money to support all my luxurious habits. The first lesson that made me aware of the shortcomings in the pursuit of money came during a family trip. My bosses would tempt us to work for months on end out of the state, or out of the country. In return for our efforts, we were awarded a weeklong paid family vacation wherever we wanted to go. I found the idea appealing. I approached my young sons (ages nine, seven, and five) and asked them to make the decision for our future family vacation. If they wanted to go to Disney World for a week, it meant that I would have to be gone for nine months. Of course, my sons wanted to go to Disney and were excited at the opportunity.

After spending the time away from my family, our weeklong vacation finally arrived. The vacation was super nice, and we had a spectacular time. But the week went by fast, too fast. On the last day, I found myself in a constant battle with my mind, grappling with this thought, "How did I ever think this was a good idea?" In my mind, I knew I had missed out watching my sons grow and learn and play for nine months. At that time, I threw away the opportunity to help my wife raise our sons. I missed out on tucking my sons into bed, helping them with their schoolwork, eating family meals together, and supporting my wife. She was left alone to do all the things that kept the house running by herself. The worst part of it all was that I let three little boys make this decision for me. Instead of being the husband, the father, and the leader, I made myself the follower. Why? Because I was consumed with having stuff. Stuff that never provided a sense of ***belonging***.

Popularity

Proverbs 11:2 (NIV), "When pride comes, then comes disgrace, but with humility comes wisdom."

My desire to be noticed is something that has taken a great number of years and multiple trials to be unrooted from me. Satan has tricked me into believing that I must be the person everyone remembers, I must be the person that leads the group, I must be the person that demonstrates his faith bigger and better than anyone else, I must be the person who flashes the biggest cross on my chest, I must carry the biggest and thickest Bible, and I must be the one who can quote the most Bible verses, I must be....etc. I was convinced for many years that I had to be the most popular, in the spotlight, up-front person in almost every area of my life, but most importantly the areas where my faith could be on display. I will probably never be able to chart the number of people I walked on or walked past to be popular.

Sometimes I attempt to think about all the people that I never spent the time to get to know because I was consumed with my own ego. I could not have possibly been that interesting. I am thankful for those who put up with my nonsense. Unfortunately, though, there is no way for me to begin to remember them all as I was caught in this space of blindness for far too long. Today, I can say that I have improved and have turned away from much of this blatant self-centeredness.

Satan will never stop attempting to devour you and me. Because of this, I have occasionally found myself still lingering in the areas of needing to be seen, to be popular, and to be the center of attention. I may not be the person who my Creator has ultimately created me to be, but I am certainly not who I was yesterday either. There are questions that always puzzle me when I think about the temptation of popularity. Did I want to **belong** to others, or did I want others to **belong** to me? Or is it simply a desire to be noticed?

The book you are reading, "Identity Matters: The Power of **Belonging**," is not the first book that I have written. My first book was titled, "How Do I Love My Neighbor, 4 Promises and 6 Truths." Many people who write books will have coordinated events where they will sell and sign their book and meet with people and talk about the book. I was very blessed to have had multiple events, of my own, after writing my book and still have many more planned. At one of these events, I was approached by a friend of mine who attends the same church. She said to me, "Why don't you have a book signing at church?"

I replied, "That is not a decision that I can make."

To which she replied, "Why don't you just ask them. That's what I would do."

Against my better judgment, I did have a conversation with a church official about planning a book signing. However, at this point, there is no clear indication as to whether or not there will ever be such an event at church. There is, however, evidence that I wanted to be noticed.

Wanting to be noticed for the first book I wrote, also took me on a journey out of state. I traveled with a couple of friends to a national conference where we thought we would pass out my book to unsuspecting people. There were many participants within the conference area, some of whom held long standing booths and some who were just visiting like me. Since the nature of this particular conference is publishing and broadcasting, there were many, many books being sold or given away. Although my friends and I did manage to share many of my books while walking through the conference, what became evident very quickly is that there were many authors who were doing the same thing as we were. Some of these authors had written dozens of books. I had a fleeting thought that I had accomplished something that would make me stand out. What I realized is that I was but a small fish in a very large pond.

Later that year, my book would provide yet another opportunity for popularity to tempt me when I would attend a retreat. This retreat was being organized by a ministry group that I am well acquainted with. In fact, I was informed long before the retreat took place that the key speakers would all be authors. For a brief moment, I did entertain a few thoughts concerning why they would not allow me to be one of the authors who would be presenting. After that day, those thoughts left me and did not return until I entered the retreat. After hearing the information presented by the authors, I quickly approached one of them and disclosed my thoughts and questions. This is what I said, "I thought that I might be one of the authors presenting this weekend, especially since I know the organizers so well. But after hearing what you shared; it is very clear to me why I am not. I could not have shared in the way that you did. All of you had very powerful presentations and I am blessed to have been present. Thank you for sharing."

It would appear to anyone reading this book that writing my first book has brought with it a constant temptation to be noticed. I cannot argue with that reasoning. Clearly, by the stories that I have shared, it is easy to see that I have not stewarded well the responsibility God provided me. Whether I was tempted to be noticed at church, at a conference, or at a retreat, I was tempted to be popular. Temptation is not what is bad, it's what you do after the temptation comes that brings the fall.

Where I find great joy is this; God asked me to write a book that I had no intention of writing. If you knew the story of how the first book came to be, you would know that it could only be by Divine design that it even exists. Somewhere in the process, I decided that I needed to be in charge of the outcome. So, for a short season, I got in the way of what God wanted to do. I have since learned to respond accordingly when God prompts me. Now the Lord has asked me to write yet another book. Praise be to God!

Psalm 100 (NIV), "Shout for joy to the Lord, all the earth. Worship the Lord with gladness; come before him with joyful songs. Know that the Lord is God It is he who made us, and we are his; we are his people, the sheep of his pasture. Enter his gates with thanksgiving and his courts with praise; give thanks to him and praise his name. For the Lord is good and his love endures forever; his faithfulness continues through all generations."

Secure

Philippians 1:6 (NIV), "being confident of this, that he who began a good work in you will carry it on to completion until the day of Christ Jesus."

It has been my experience that many Christians never discover their true gifting. The gifting that makes each of us unique and different is the blessing that God places on your life. Your gifting is, in essence, your contribution to His kingdom. The main reason most people never uncover their true gifting is because they don't realize that everyone has intrinsic value, no one person is more important than another. Some people have gifts that stand out, like a pastor, while others are not as noticeable, like someone who is a helper or an encourager. We live in a world that places little value on the things of God and greater value on the things of the world. Our world also would have us think that our worth is solely based on our performance, our possessions, and what other people think about us. None of those worldly things will ever provide **belonging**. Only God can give that to you.

Sometimes, we attain a level of spirituality that tricks us into thinking we have discovered the gifting that God has called us to. Our gifting is truly who God made us to be and if we are walking in it, we should never grow weary, never lose interest, and never compare ourselves to others. If we do any of those things, we are probably not walking in our God-given gifting. We may be walking in some ministry that we decided we preferred better? But we are not walking in our natural God-given gifting. Whenever we strive in our own strength, we will undoubtedly begin to quickly lose interest in what we are doing. If we are walking in the gifting God has blessed us with it is a natural extension of who we are and we shall never grow weary. Understanding our gifting allows us to walk in our identity as God's children. Finally, this is important, because without knowing who we are and "Whose" we are, we will never experience a deep **belonging**. Again, as we walk further in faith, our **belonging** is strengthened.

I remember a season when I thought I was secure in who I was and "Whose" I was. My identity, my gifting, and my **belonging** were firmly established, and growing. The church that I attend announced that there would be additional positions opening soon for a particular ministry. In my mind, I thought that I would be a great candidate for one of the available positions. So, I threw my name into the ring. In fact, I asked several of my friends to nominate me as well. The outcome of this decision did not end up the way that I had hoped. But after a brief season of wallowing in self-pity, God would make His presence known to me in a way that He had not done before. This trial would move my faith to levels that I did not know were possible. In the end, my identity, my gifting, and my **belonging** all grew to new heights as I learned a great lesson and was pulled closer to God.

When I was initially contacted as a candidate, I was excited at the possibility. But to my surprise, after one week I was informed, through voicemail, that I was no longer a candidate. I returned the call to the church representative and thanked them for the consideration and the opportunity. Then I asked, "What is it that I don't know about myself, and how can I grow from this experience?"

To this, the church representative stated, "That's a really great question. Unfortunately, I don't have an answer for you. Thanks for getting back to me. Goodbye." At first, I was alright with the exchange, but very quickly my pride was wounded, and I thought that more information should have been afforded to me. So, I called the church representative once again.

When she answered, I stated, "I think there is a misunderstanding here. When I asked you what is it that I didn't know about myself and how can I grow from this experience, I did not ask for someone else's personal information or for some secret inside church information. However, you gave me nothing anyway."

This time the church representative was very stern and asked, "What is it you think I owe you?"

I replied, "You don't owe me anything. I didn't think I was talking to a Fortune 500 company. I thought I was talking to the church. There must be something about me that does not meet your requirements or else why did you remove me as a candidate. Perhaps, I will never possess the gifts, talents, or credentials that you are looking for in this position. Since we have never met and all you have is a piece of paper in front of you with my name on it, I can only assume that this was all political theatre as you already knew who you wanted for the positions. I wonder how many other people you have treated with such disregard. I must have been mistaken to think the church would lead the charge in the way we should treat people. I guess, I thought, I would receive better from you than that. My mistake!"

At this, she stated once again, "Sir, you are no longer a candidate. Thank you."

For almost three weeks, I was angered, hurt, bitter, wounded, and offended. Virtually every moment of every day I was scrutinizing the conversation I had had with the church representative in my mind. I was so appalled that the church could treat people this way. I was so angry, I was so hurt, I was so bitter, I was so wounded, and I was so offended that I was ready to leave the church. I had conversations with multiple people about my considerations and felt like at any moment I would walk away. My constant thoughts were, "If this is how the church functions and treats people, how was I so deceived into believing that this was the right place to worship God? Furthermore, if this is what the church looks like behind the scenes, is there a church anywhere that could provide an honest and true image of Christ?" My mind was reeling incessantly.

Still in my agitated and angered state, I attended DIG, my Tuesday morning Bible study. During the summer months, we used to take a break from the Bible and instead we would watch topical Bible videos. That morning, at the DIG Bible study, almost three weeks into the heat of my thoughts of separation, God spoke to me as clearly as He had ever done before. But this time, instead of simply providing a gradual transformation, there was also an immediate effect.

The video began and the pastor who was presenting the information told a story of how he had to preside over the funerals of two men the previous week. He shared that one of the men was only 18 years old and had not been given the time to make a deep impact on the world. But the other man was 80. The pastor told the people in the audience, "This man most of you probably knew. He probably married some of you. He probably buried some of your loved ones. He probably prayed with many of you. He probably visited many of you in the hospital. He probably visited many of you in your homes. He probably ministered to many of you during the difficult seasons of life. This man has silently lived among us for decades and he has left an impression that will not be soon forgotten. Finally, this man was probably a better pastor than I could ever hope to be."

At that moment, God said to me so clearly, "That is who I created you to be Jeff. That is who you are!"

Promptly! Instantaneously! Immediately, in the snap of a finger, the weight of my anger, my hurt, my bitterness, my wound, and my offense were lifted off my shoulders. My breathing and countenance were heightened. God had wholly redeemed and restored me through the refining fire of my trial of offense. I will never forget that day. More importantly, I will never forget that moment. What is probably the most amazing outcome from that day is that I have yet to be offended again. God solidified my identity, my gifting, and my **belonging** so much so that it has penetrated the core of my being. The security of who I am and "Whose" I am will always grow, but it was firmly planted in me that day.

Additionally, God clarified a few more things to me about that circumstance in the weeks following. First, the desire to be a candidate for one of the positions in the church was my desire, not God's. Second, I was protected from having to function in a space that would not be conducive to my gifting and calling. Last, God reminded me that even the church is flawed, in some cases more so than we might believe, because it is run by humans. So, God brought me to a passage from the Prophet Hosea and there I pondered deeply what He had done.

Hosea 3:1 (NIV), 'The Lord said to me, "Go, show your love to your wife again, though she is loved by another man and is an adulteress. Love her as the Lord loves the Israelites, though they turn to other gods and love the sacred raisin cakes."'

Embraced

Colossians 3:14 (NIV), "And over all these virtues put on love, which binds them all together in perfect unity."

I received a request from a person who needed someone to perform a funeral. I called the number provided and a woman answered. She stated that her father-in-law had died and wanted to know if I would come to the family's house and sit with them to discuss the details of their father's service. Of course, I obliged. When I arrived, I sat down at the kitchen table with the family members. Before we began to discuss their deceased father/husband, each of them introduced themselves to me. The woman I spoke with on the phone said, "I am the daughter-in-law, and this is my partner. We love your church." Her partner said, "I am the daughter, and I am her wife. I will second that, we love your church."

The mother said, "I am the widow. I am angry at God, and I am angry at the church. My husband never felt like he was accepted by the church. Now there is no way to make it right by him."

The son said, "I am the son. I am an atheist. I don't care about your church, and I don't care about your god. All I ask is that you do right by my father." After I listened to the family introduce themselves, there were many thoughts running through my mind. However, none was more important than this one, "God, I need You! Please be with us in these moments. I have no idea how I will meet the needs of these people. Only You can do this. Thank You!"

I spent nearly an hour listening to the family members speak about the life of their loved one. As you might expect, there were many memories and fond moments. To me, this part of my service is always very special. I get to learn about people from a unique perspective. Almost always, the family lets down their guard and begins to laugh and cry, at will, as they share and remember their loved ones. Many times, I find myself crying with them. When I left the house, each family member hugged me, even the atheist. God must have intervened, as there was surely no way that I was going to be able to meet each person in their grief knowing that they all come from a vastly different perspective. I recalled a book that I read years earlier and thought about some of the passages. Here is what I remember from it.

"Spiritual direction is difficult. Pastoral wisdom is not available on prescription. Every person who comes to a pastor with a heart full of shapeless longings and a head full of badgering questions is complex in a new way. People need someone who is secure enough to absorb, reflect, and tolerate every despair and temptation, and strong enough to do something for them. Even if that is only to provide space for the Holy Spirit to initiate new life. There is no fail-proof formulae. For a start, I can cultivate an attitude of awe. I must be prepared to marvel. This face

before me, its loveliness scored with stress, is in the image of God. The significance I see before me is not what I see before me but what Christ has said and done. This is a person for whom Christ died, a person He loves: an awesome fact! Am I prepared to admire? Am I prepared to respect? Am I prepared to be in reverence? Every meeting with another person is a privilege. In pastoral conversation I have chances that many never get as easily or as frequently—chances to spy out suppressed glory, ignored blessing, forgotten grace. I had better not miss them. I take with absolute seriousness whatever part I play, but I am a supporting player and not the lead. I do my very best, but in no way do I speak or act so that a person's response to me is the center-stage action. God wants to meet with this person. I must not manipulate the conversation or construe the setting so that I am perceived to be in charge, or I merely delay the things of God. If I dominate the conversation, either ignoring God's word and presence and mercy or consigning him to merely ceremonial position, then I am getting in the way. This cannot be reduced to procedure or formula." (Eugene Peterson, Working the Angles)

When the funeral service was complete, all the family members embraced me. I make a habit of waiting for the family in the adjoining parlor after every funeral I perform. I believe it's important to provide one last offering to the grieving family, just to make sure that all their needs are met. At this funeral, the woman who I spoke with initially met me in the parlor to thank me again. She then disclosed that she was raised in a conservative home under a conservative, almost strict, religion and that she wasn't always a lesbian. Pursuing this lifestyle, although hard, was what she believed made her whole. She thanked me yet again. To which I replied, "You are welcome."

She said, "You don't understand. My childhood church won't even have conversations with me and my partner. You have made us feel welcome in your presence. You can't know how huge that is!" We hugged again and I left. I don't know if this family felt any sense of **belonging** as each of them has such a varied view of the world. I do know they were extremely appreciative as they sent a letter to the church expressing their gratitude. What I am absolutely sure of is this, I **belong** to God, and He created me to be with *all* people and give away what I have received. Everyone wants to **belong**, lets invite them into that.

Direction

Isaiah 40:31 (NIV), "but those who hope in the Lord will renew their strength. They will soar on wings like eagles; they will run and not grow weary, they will walk and not be faint."

Throughout my faith journey, there always seemed to be a man or two who would emerge from nowhere and enter my circumstance. When I look back at all the seasons of my life, that was always the case. Not until I found a bit of maturity, did I even take a moment to notice. I have often wondered from where these people came. But as you begin to see God more clearly and understand your faith more intimately, you begin to realize that the promises of Scripture are true. God is working on your behalf because He is crazy about you. He will send these people, mostly men in my case, at just the right time to help you and guide you. That feeling of being embraced by God brings with it a profound sense of **belonging**.

The first man God brought was John Ribbing. John was the leader of my first small group Bible study. He and his wife Karen demonstrated what God could do both in your faith and in your marriage. John knew exactly what words to say and what topics to focus on when we were talking. He also knew exactly how to support the men of the group when trials and tribulations arose. John and Karen also lead their children in the godliest of ways and provided everyone in the group with a sense of family. This married couple graced the presence of many people as they hosted small group after small group in their home. I remember John encouraging me to begin my own small group after spending three or four Bible studies under his guidance. I will never forget the Ribbings as my **belonging** began to strengthen while under their care.

Jeff Wolf, Ed Nightingale, and Joe Patrico were three men who stood out in a time when God knew that I needed encouragement and a scriptural foundation. These men poured themselves into me for years. Next, God brought Randy Wolyniec, Randy Yates, Dave Lupek, Larry Barnes, and Ed Sprock. These men taught me about life, family, serving, giving, and seeing the world through unbiased eyes. They showed me what it meant to give selflessly. They surrounded me and lifted me higher than I thought I could go. God also brought men such as Steve Buckner, John Burket, Fred Covyeau, Tom Hoag, Dave Nicholas, and Jerry McCloud. Each of these men sharpened me through God's Word and they drove my eyes toward Jesus. They helped me to experience a bigger glimpse of His love. God also brought men who demonstrated the art of loving and caring for people in ministry such as Kevin Samov, Rick David, and Chris Cook. These men are experts in seeing the hurt and pain in any room and then responding accordingly. I have been blessed by their fellowship.

Al Beahn walked into my life and for the first time I was joined by someone who could walk with me through similar circumstances. Al demonstrated a willingness to "let go" and "let God." He did not have all the answers, but he was certain that God was at the end of every question. Most importantly, Al was willing to share his life with me. We spent hours, week after week, learning, growing, laughing, crying, loving, hurting, and healing. Most importantly, we did it together. Al is the man who showed me how to navigate the most profoundly difficult relationship challenges. It was as if he was saying to me, "Follow my lead. If God can get me through this, He can certainly get you through it as well." Al loves me. He loves me so much, in fact, when he knew it was time for me to soar even higher, he introduced me to a man who could take me higher. Then Al graciously stepped out into the background, thus demonstrating his distinct humility.

Men such as Basil Denno, David Strubler, Bill Wampler, and Steve Wentzel were most willing to help me tackle the deep and probing questions about God. Each of these men in their own unique gifting provided insight through prayer and council. Craig Mayes, Erik Bledsoe, Danny Cox, Chris Zarbaugh, James Friedman, Donearl Johnson, Dave Halsey, and Tim Morton are great leaders of men. They have challenged me to see the gospel and Jesus through the purest of eyes. Their readiness to stretch themselves for the kingdom, to be ambassadors in every aspect, to let their lives be a visible demonstration of obedience for God has inspired me to continue to grow. Woman like Rita Witchner taught me how to become effective in prayer. Stephanie Valentine and Melodie Kondratek helped me grow in ministry leadership, while walking beside me instilling their own unique gifts. Barb Bakotich welcomed me into a bigger piece of the kingdom and allowed me to lead and guide. Sonja Maletta demonstrated servant leadership by loving people better than anyone I know. Sonja walks this earth, Spirit led with no walls on her gospel. Her leadership is unmatched.

Seth Vandervleight has loved me and shown me how to walk in the Spirit. God has used Seth to reveal Himself to me in a most powerful way. Seth has always been a faithful vessel. Whenever there is something troubling my spirit, I tend to receive a phone call from my friend Seth. Once, while we were on the phone, I was recalling a time when I was still blind and caught in legalism. I was thanking Seth for helping me to see, and Seth said something that I will never forget.

Seth said, "Jeff, you didn't even know you were blind." Seth didn't demand anything of me, he simply loved me. Because of Seth, I now know a deeper grace and that I am the beloved.

Steve Andrews has allowed me space in his life. His schedule is always very demanding, but he always seems to find the time. Steve's life is such a rich history of faith. He has been blessed by God in ways that I may never know. But Steve allows me to see through his experience. He points me to places that I did not know existed. Steve is gracious, kind, and humble. I am certainly a better man because of him. Ron Daggett is a man of faith with very little room for nonsense. If you want to know, or see, what a great steward of faith is, you only need to spend a short time with Ron to know that his life could be summed up in this way; God first, God second, God always. His wisdom and discernment are truly gifts from God. Because Ron is so wise, he has the ability to cut to the heart of any matter quickly. Whenever I sit with Ron, I always walk away with a nugget or two of wisdom.

Few things are more satisfying than sensing that you are favored, that you are loved and known by someone; someone sees your soul and they delight in you; they believe in you, and they believe what you do will change lives. This is what you will receive if you have the pleasure of meeting my friend and mentor, Loren Siffring. Loren has fathered me when I needed it. He has loved me always. He provides strength, encouragement, understanding, patience, and spiritual direction. No man in my life has been more influential than Loren. He is a gift from God. In fact, when I had yet to meet Loren, I kept hearing his name being mentioned by others during conversations. My prayer partner, friend, and mentor Al Beahn decided that I should meet Loren, so he introduced us. Meeting Loren has proven to be one of the greatest days of my life. I don't know who I would be without Loren's ability to help me see clearly. Loren's understanding of Jesus and his depiction of discipleship is more than beautiful, it's awe-inspiring.

Many of the aforementioned people, I still have the pleasure of walking with consistently. All of them are still friends and mentors. All of them have contributed to my understanding of who I am, Whose I am, and the deepening of my ***belonging***. I know, with great certainty, that if needed, I could call any one of them, and we would find a time to sit down and talk through whatever trial, struggle, decision, or joyous event that may come. There are no words that would adequately describe the impact each of these people have had on my life. I walk with profound joy because of what God has done. All these people were God sent.

Hebrews 13:7 (NIV), "Remember your leaders, who spoke the word of God to you. Consider the outcome of their way of life and imitate their faith."

Called

Romans 8:28 (NIV), "And we know that in all things God works for the good of those who love him, who have been called according to his purpose."

I have been called many times to visit people in the hospital. Part of my gifting from God is to be with people in their most difficult days. I gain a stronger sense of ***belonging*** every time I make a visit. Every time I am called, even after more than 1,000 visits, I always get a little nervous before I enter the room. As I approach, I pray that God will be the One the patient sees, and I will not get in the way. I am so thankful for the nervous reaction within me because it causes me to be mindful that I am God's vessel. Sometimes, however, I get nervous even before I leave my house. This happens when the circumstances of the patient, prior to my visit, have been handled poorly. On one such visit, a man from my church was besieged with advanced cancer. The doctors predicted he only had days to live. He was unresponsive because his body was shutting down. His small group asked the church to send someone, but the message was mishandled and never passed on to the correct person. Unfortunately, this mishandling occurred four more times over the next several days.

When the request was finally given to me, it came with a warning. The verbal warning was, "Be mindful of the environment." I was told that there were many family members who have loudly shared their displeasure because of the length of time it had taken for the church to make a visit. More than that, I was told that the man who was dying and his wife were Christians who had both been previously divorced. Both the man and his wife had adult children and none of them were Christians. The adult children were the family members who were displeased with the lack of response from the church. In fact, they were atheists and were grilling their mother in the hospital making these statements, "This is the God you worship? This is how your church shows up for you when you are in trouble? This is the treatment you expect to receive from your tithing? This is the community you keep raving about? Sign us up! We can't wait to join this group. Sounds like great fun!" Now you can begin to understand why I was nervous before I left my house. The environment was challenging to say the least.

When I arrived at the hospital, the man's wife was the first person I encountered. She quickly filled me in on the status of her husband and then walked me to the place where her and her husband's children were gathered. All the couple's children were huddled together in a circle, and I was thrust into everyone's presence at once. We walked into the father's room, and I asked if we could all pray together. To my surprise, no one hesitated. I don't remember the words that I shared other than asking God for a quick and painless transition. I can't even tell you if the words carried more weight than my being *with* them while their father was still alive.

Before leaving the hospital, I sat with the couple's children outside their father's room. None of them were condescending. I did not sense any angst. They were caught in grief. What seemed to matter to them more than anything else, was someone showed up. Someone finally showed up. Because they were atheists, I could easily assume they would resist my presence. But I have come to understand that there are no atheists in a fox hole. These people wanted what was best for their dying father. God provided the courage and strength that I needed to walk into a potentially hostile environment. What these people wanted was someone to be *with* them. That day God chose me as His instrument of peace.

On another occasion, I was called by a woman who asked if I could visit her husband because he was battling Leukemia. She asked if I could spend some time with him as he was angry and depressed because of his circumstances. I agreed to visit her husband and invited my friend Rick to come along with me. What we did not know was that the wife never informed her husband that we were coming to see him. That would prove to be very interesting as the husband did not want visitors. When we arrived, the man was reluctant to speak to us and was extremely reserved. He managed to tell us about his affliction and his anger towards God. At first, his demeanor was staunch and calculated, but slowly his countenance began to soften. Rick and I encouraged him. We reminded him how valuable he was in God's eyes. We painted the vision of his return to work and the demonstration that his faith would portray to his fellow workers, and how he could shine the light of Christ amid calamities. Finally, Rick and I shared how encouraged we both were because of his strength and willingness to carry on despite Leukemia. At this the man started to cry. We could not help but to cry with him. Then we ended our visit with prayer. In less than an hour, God completely altered the man's view of his condition and opened his eyes to greater possibilities for his future. Rick and I were able to witness this firsthand. The roots of my ***belonging*** grow deeper each time God calls me.

-Lessons Learned-

Many of the ills of our world stem from our turning away from God. There is untold devastation occurring all around us because we have lost the value of God's Word and His Righteousness. The family unit has been maligned. Many men and women no longer understand their roles and how to lead their families well. True discipleship is a lost art. Satan and our culture have convinced many that it is better to live separate than in community. Most of us, even those who claim to be Christian, can't find ***belonging***. If we can't find ***belonging***, how are we planning to give ***belonging*** to anyone else? Many of us have found our identity in a god of the world instead of God Almighty, Maker of Heaven and Earth. When we finally get to the point when we have had enough, we usually end up accomplishing nothing more than placing a band-aid on a bullet hole instead of solving a problem. We need to slow down, look around, and find God again. We need God! We need Jesus! We need the Holy Spirit!

1 Corinthians 3:23 (NLT), "and you belong to Christ, and Christ belongs to God."

7

Knowing is Everything!

Matthew 7:7-8 (NIV), "Ask and it will be given to you; seek and you will find; knock and the door will be opened to you. For everyone who asks receives; the one who seeks finds; and to the one who knocks, the door will be opened."

I set out at a very early age to find answers to why my childhood was filled with divorce and brokenness. I spoke with anyone who would listen. I desperately wanted to attach an answer to the question, "Where do I **belong**?" The determination to continually search for an answer that made sense was probably the catalyst for my finding God along the way as it lines up with His Word and His promises. God has illuminated my path and guided me to a greater understanding of life, my relationships, and my purpose. He has revealed to me the gifting and calling He has placed on my life. He has forever cemented my identity in Him. I know that I **belong** to Him. If I did not find God, I am certain that I would still be lost and searching. God has taken every crooked thing and made it straight again.

Luke 3:5 (NIV), "Every valley shall be filled in, every mountain and hill made low. The crooked roads shall become straight, the rough ways smooth."

When we begin our walk with God, there is no end to the things we can find to keep us busy, working for the Lord. We are filled with excitement, and we wander aimlessly from task to task believing God needs us to perform. We are short on obedience as it is not a word that registers with our faith. We are too busy living as human *doings* instead of as human *beings*. Later in our journey, we advance in spirituality and gradually our actions diminish. This decrease in action continues until we are filled with obedience.

At this point, God can begin to mold us into the person He created us to be. We begin to see that our gifting and calling is as natural to us as breathing. This is because God knows what He is doing. We no longer have dreams of standing in front of thousands to share a message, nor do we wish to build schools or drill water wells in foreign lands. Our thoughts of comparing ourselves to others vanish, hidden behind the intrinsic value we feel through the eyes of our Heavenly Father. We no longer want to do anything that our Heavenly Father doesn't ask of us. This is because we know we *belong* to Him. When His opinion is the only one that matters, we grow to become unoffendable.

{Unoffendable}

Acts 24:16 (KJV), "And herein do I exercise myself, to have always a conscience void of offence toward God, and toward men."

Hebrews 13:18 (NIV), "Pray for us. We are sure that we have a clear conscience and desire to live honorably in every way."

When we are obedient to God, He can then send us out into more difficult and challenging circumstances as His representative. He entrusts us with this great responsibility because we have exercised our conscience to be "unoffendable." This does not mean that we can no longer be offended, it simply means that we can sense an offense welling up inside us and refuse to give it life. We will not allow our emotions to get in the way of the things of God or to delay the things of God. We know that we *belong* to Him, and He *alone* is responsible for any outcome that may ensue. There are many assurances that come with an unoffendable conscience. We will always leave people no worse than we found them as it is not us, but the Holy Spirit that is guiding us. We are His chosen instrument, His vessel, and always the reflector of His light. We would not want any unrighteous behavior on our part, to jeopardize our ability to proclaim His goodness because our words and actions are not in alignment. Remaining unoffendable requires constant and daily exercise. It is not a place that we can arrive, but with constant exercise, or practice, we can retain.

Colossians 1:27-29 (NIV), "To them God has chosen to make known among the Gentiles the glorious riches of this mystery, which is Christ in you, the hope of glory. He is the one we proclaim, admonishing and teaching everyone with all wisdom, so that we may present everyone fully mature in Christ. To this end I strenuously contend with all the energy Christ so powerfully works in me."

Christ is our hope of glory. How powerfully would we allow Christ to work in us? Would we allow Christ to remove every wall from our preconceived gospel? Would we allow Him to present us fully mature? Would we love others as He has loved us? Would we give Him the title Lord? **Lord** declares the position Jesus holds in your life, whereas **Savior** describes what He has done for you. We cannot partake of the benefit of His sacrifice unless we come under His position as Lord and King! We must spend our days on this earth pointing each other to Jesus.

Romans 5:6 (NIV), "You see, at just the right time, when we were still powerless, Christ died for the ungodly."

Have you ever had a moment or a series of moments when you realized that there was nothing you did to create them? If you have, how often have they occurred? These are the moments along our journey where we acknowledge we have seen and experienced things that are beyond anything we can create on our own. God's supremacy is made visible in us and through us. It's as if we have been made for this purpose. In those moments we have reached the completeness of happiness, and our desire for *belonging* is fulfilled. Just as the taste of the Lord is good, so too is every new moment we experience living in the goodness and awareness of God's perfect love. We become more eager to have more of Jesus living inside us, because we *belong* to Him. When we come to the realization that we are His and He holds all things together we begin to understand that God is bigger than our minds can comprehend. Every time He reveals something new to us, we see that our understanding was grossly limited. In other words, the more we know of God the more we realize what we don't know of God. We will never gain ground on the One who created all things as our *belonging* continues to deepen.

There is a hymn titled, "Now I *Belong* to Jesus." It's a reminder of the ultimate *belonging* you can experience with your Lord and Savior Jesus Christ. Verse 3 reads, "Joy floods my soul, for Jesus has saved me, freed me from sin that long had enslaved me; His precious blood He gave to redeem. Now I ***belong*** to Him." There is no greater confidence than knowing you ***belong*** to Jesus for all eternity!

Have you made a commitment to Christ so that you can say that you ***belong*** to him? Experience the greatest sense of ***belonging*** possible through new life in Him when you ask Him to become your Lord and Savior. Then you will say, "Now I ***belong*** to Him!"

Maranatha

Philippians 4:6-7 (NIV), "Do not be anxious about anything, but in every situation, by prayer and petition, with thanksgiving, present your requests to God. And the peace of God, which transcends all understanding, will guard your hearts and your minds in Christ Jesus."

One year, my mentor was organizing a men's retreat. Anyone attending would be traveling nearly four hours to a Christian camp called "Maranatha Bible and Missionary Conference" in Muskegon, Michigan. When I found out the date of this trip I began to plan. I invited two men to travel with me to Maranatha as I knew they would benefit from attending. Mike agreed to attend, almost immediately, while Phil said "no" numerous times. As the retreat was drawing near, I repeatedly asked Phil to come along. Each time, Phil denied my offer. Finally, less than a week before the retreat, I told Phil, "Have your bag packed on Friday afternoon, because I will be picking you up so you can attend the retreat. I have already paid your way." Finally, Phil agreed.

Mike was eager to attend because he was getting ready to launch his own ministry, called "The C4 Initiative" (small men's retreats built on discipleship), later that year with a group of men. Mike wanted to watch someone share a series of messages so he could gain some perspective for himself. He was responsible for delivering the weekend messages at the upcoming C4 retreat. Phil, on the other hand, was reluctant because God had already started him on a journey of discovery, and he was not sure the Maranatha retreat was the direction God was calling him. God asked Phil to "step out of the boat" some months earlier and Phil needed some prodding.

When I asked several times and then paid his entry fee, Phil saw it as a sign he should go.

I was working on editing the audio version of my first book, "How Do I Love My Neighbor" in the days leading up to the retreat. On the Tuesday evening before the retreat, I received a phone call from Gabe, the young man who was helping with the editing process of my book. However, I was unable to answer it. On the Wednesday morning, two days before we left for Maranatha, I found out that another family had lost a child, and their daughter's funeral was that day. I asked a third party for the phone number of the parents and sent the text message that I had received on the day of my son's funeral, "I have a license to talk to you. Today I will begin praying for you. When you are ready, I will be here." To my surprise, they invited me to attend. When the formal part of the service was complete, it was announced that the microphone would remain open for anyone who might want to share a few kind words. I kept feeling prodded by God to get up and speak, but my flesh would not let me do it. I was not very happy with myself. I remember leaving the funeral with a sense of unrest.

On the morning we were to leave for the retreat, I had to visit the eye doctor to have a non-invasive procedure completed. When I exited the freeway, on the way to the eye doctor, I was stopped at the traffic light at the top of the ramp. Out of the corner of my eye, I could see there was a homeless man sitting on a chair at the traffic light. I did not want to look in his direction. That is when God asked, "Are you really not going to roll down the window?" At this, I rolled down the window and offered the homeless man some cash and said, "God bless you." Twice in two days I had been apprehensive, almost unresponsive to the leadings of God. To say that I was not happy with myself is an understatement. After my appointment, Mike, Phil, and I were finally in the car enroute to Maranatha.

On Friday evening, we heard the first of five messages and then we were off to the fire pit for some fellowship. I went to my room to get my folding (bag) chair so I could sit around the fire. Before I left my room, my phone beeped indicating that I had received a voicemail. When I listened to it, I found out that it came from Gabe, the young man who is helping with the editing process of my audio book. He called on Tuesday evening, and for some reason my voicemail had been delayed almost three days. When I listened to it, he said, "I was at the section of your book when Hank sent you the text message at your son's funeral. I wanted you to know that we have close family friends who have just lost a daughter. The mom's name is Rita. I was wondering if you would reach out to them and help them through this most difficult time?" To my wonder, I thought, "How is this possible? My voicemail was delayed two days. The message from Gabe informed me of a funeral of a child. It was the same funeral I had attended two days prior. How wonderful that God would prompt Gabe to reach out to me, knowing that I needed to be at the funeral! Only God could do such things!"

Mike, Phil, and I would receive some valuable teachings over that weekend. Mike was able to witness a man compose multiple complimentary messages during the retreat. He was able to briefly speak to the presenter before we left Maranatha to gain additional knowledge about building one message on top of another. Phil was sitting in a quiet time of meditation on Sunday morning when God spoke to him through a series of fallen acorns. He realized that he had gotten in front of God and was making his journey more difficult than it needed to be. With Phil's newfound perspective, he knew the direction God was leading him, and was eager to put his wisdom into action. On the drive home, each of us shared the revelation that God had provided while we were at Maranatha. We praised the Lord all the way home.

The following week, Phil reached out to a friend who owned a local restaurant and set his new direction in motion. I went back to business as usual but armed with the new knowledge from the retreat. Almost two months later, Mike and the guys from C4 Initiative conducted their first retreat. Everything went well for them, especially the messages that Mike had learned to deliver in succession. Ten weeks after the Maranatha retreat, Mike attended the Tuesday morning DIG Bible study. Mike had a brand-new Bible in his hand, and I asked if I could take a look at it. Examining the Bible, I noticed that it was bendable, the leather was soft, the font was crisp and clear, and that there were not many footnotes, almost none. I own many Bibles and there was no reason for me to purchase another one. But for some reason, I had to have this particular Bible, so I ordered it.

When it arrived a few days later, I removed the Bible from its sleeve and opened it up. It randomly opened to the end of 1 Corinthians. My eyes were drawn to the "Final Greetings" section of the 16th chapter. When I reached verse 22, which reads:

1 Corinthians 16:22 (NIV), "If anyone does not love the Lord, let that person be cursed! Come, Lord!"

I was struggling to understand the complexity of it. So, I paused for a few minutes. I thought, "Why is this verse so perplexing to me?" Then I looked back at this page of the Bible and found there was a footnote for verse 22. It read, "The *Greek* for "Come, Lord" reproduces an Aramaic expression (Maranatha) used by early Christians." It was now more than 10 weeks after our retreat, and God was still speaking to me. Only You God! Only You can do such things! This is another example of how God has grown, strengthened, and deeply rooted my ***belonging***. He continues to do so. Every time He does this, He provides further evidence that I am His. I am His beloved. I ***belong*** to Him. Praise be to God!

Wine

Psalm 32:8 (NIV), "I will instruct you and teach you in the way you should go; I will counsel you with my loving eye on you."

One Sunday after church, I was running behind because I had provided some extended prayer time with a few of the parishioners. When I realized that I had misjudged my time and probably had not left myself enough time to meet my other two commitments, I began to panic. I thought, "Maybe I should cancel the hospital visit? By eliminating the hospital visit, that should all but guarantee that I would arrive on time for the premarital classes I was providing later that day." Hospital visits are important to me, especially knowing that the patients are counting on your commitment to come and visit them. So, I decided that I would rush to the hospital and make a short visit as promised.

Upon entering the hospital, I happened to bump into the young lady who trained our dog, her name is Lauren. I said, "Hello Lauren. It's so nice to see you. Oh no! If I am seeing you in the hospital, that must mean someone is not doing well."

Lauren responded, "Yes, my mother is struggling with cancer and things are looking rather bleak."

I asked "Lauren, do you think it would be all right if I made a visit to your mom's room?"

She said, "That would be wonderful."

I said to Lauren, "I will make the visit with your mother tomorrow as I am in a bit of a time crunch." I immediately went to the patient's room that I promised to visit. When I arrived, there was no one in the room. I asked a nurse if she knew where the patient was, and the nurse said that they were in the lab for testing and would not return for 45 minutes. So, I rushed on to my premarital class meeting.

I returned to the hospital the next day, and my first visit was to the patient that I had promised previously. After spending some quality time with him, I made my way to Lauren's mom Cheryl's room. When I arrived at Cheryl's room, it was immediately apparent to me that she was in the late stages of cancer. I could see that her husband had been living in the room with her and her demeanor was run-down. I introduced myself and after a brief conversation, we discovered that they were neighbors with some friends of mine. Cheryl shared her journey through cancer and how she finally ended up at the hospital.

Then she told me that she was going home in the next day or two. She knew that the hospital was only prolonging the inevitable and she wanted to be home with family and friends for whatever time she had left. When she shared this, I could hear a mix of emotions in her voice. She sounded excited to be going home but at the same time fearful for the outcome and not knowing exactly how long she would live. At the end of my stay with her, I asked, "Cheryl, can I pray for you?"

She stated, "I am not very religious, but why would I deny myself prayer. Sure, please do!"

When I was about to leave, I asked Cheryl, "Would you like me to make a home visit?"

At this, Cheryl became tearful, and she asked, "You would make a house call? You would come to my house and do that?"

I responded, "Cheryl, I would be happy to make a house visit. Your daughter extended my family such warm kindness while she was training our dog, I would love to shower you with the same kindness."

When I arrived at Cheryl's house to make my visit, I was quite surprised at Cheryl's demeanor. It appeared to have changed for the better and she had a glow about her. She was lying on a hospital bed in the living room and stated that she had a couple of requests she wanted to ask of me. Walt, Cheryl's husband, and her daughter Lauren helped Cheryl to a sitting position and Cheryl made her first request. She asked, "Would you be willing to come back, one more time, when all my family is present and pray for me? I would like all the people I love to be here, and we could have sort of a good-bye vigil. Would you be willing to preside over that for me?"

I said, "Cheryl, I am your servant. I am willing to do whatever you ask of me."

Then she said, "My second request is this, would you perform my funeral?"

I responded, "I would be honored. It would be my pleasure." Cheryl let me know that ever since I prayed with her in the hospital, she had been thinking about asking these requests of me. She mentioned that she believed in God but had not attended church in a very long time, and if I said "no" she did not know what she would do. I thanked her for thinking of me. A couple of days later everyone Cheryl had requested gathered in her living room for a time of prayer. We shared some deeply emotional conversations, and many tears fell. Good-byes were offered to everyone as Cheryl did not want to take the chance that she might not be able to say good-bye later. I departed and waited for the call.

Less than a week later, I was informed that Cheryl was gone and was provided her funeral arrangements. The family requested both a Mausoleum service as well as a grave-side service. I was more than happy to accommodate them. They also requested that I attend Cheryl's celebration luncheon and say a few words. It was to be held at a wine tasting venue because Cheryl was a wine connoisseur. I agreed to that as well. When the time came for me to share my thoughts about Cheryl, I let everyone know that I would be directing them to the first recorded miracle of Jesus.

John 2:1-11 (NIV), 'On the third day a wedding took place at Cana in Galilee. Jesus' mother was there, and Jesus and his disciples had also been invited to the wedding. When the wine was gone, Jesus' mother said to him, "They have no more wine." "Woman, why do you involve me?" Jesus replied. "My hour has not yet come." His mother said to the servants, "Do whatever he tells you." Nearby stood six stone water jars, the kind used by the Jews for ceremonial washing, each holding from twenty to thirty gallons. Jesus said to the servants, "Fill the jars with water"; so they filled them to the brim. Then he told them, "Now draw some out and take it to the master of the banquet." They did so, and the master of the banquet tasted the water that had been turned into wine. He did not realize where it had come from, though the servants who had drawn the water knew. Then he called the bridegroom aside and said, "Everyone brings out the choice wine first and then the cheaper wine after the guests have had too much to drink; but you have saved the best till now." What Jesus did here in Cana of Galilee was the first of the signs through which he revealed his glory; and his disciples believed in him.'

I closed my time with these words, "Cheryl is the reason we gather here today. Let us always remember the person she was and the way that she loved. She was a connoisseur of wine, which is why we have assembled in this place. Unlike fine wine, which takes time to mature the palate, before we can appreciate it, Cheryl was vastly different. Because once you met Cheryl, there was no need to mature your palate, you knew immediately that you liked her. May she rest in peace."

The events of this story almost didn't happen. If I had not taken the time to fulfill my commitment to make a hospital visit, this story does not come to life. This is just another way that God continues to show me He is with me, and He is faithful. The circumstances of stories like this develop when I am not aware. God cultivates fresh new ways of showing me who He is and removing any doubt that I **belong** to Him. Is there any better place to **belong**? I think not!

Book

Matthew 19:26 (NIV), 'Jesus looked at them and said, "With man this is impossible, but with God all things are possible."'

On a Sunday morning in January of 2020, God spoke to me and said I was to write a book. I was excited because I had never written a book before, nor did I ever have plans to write a book. The contents of the book were all in my head, and I thought that I would have it written in a couple of weeks. However, that is not what happened. I would quickly find out that writing a book is a bit of a journey. Along the journey, God kept making His presence known which made it impossible for me to think that I had conjured up this idea by myself. From the people He surrounded me with, to the stories that filled the book, to the publisher who printed it, God was always there.

When the book was finally written and the bulk of the editing was nearly completed, the main editor, my friend Judy, said to me, "Now you need some reviews."

To which I replied, "I have no idea what you just said. What is a review?"

Judy stated, "A review is a couple of sentences that depict the significance of the book by a notable or a famous person."

I said, "Judy, I don't know anyone famous."

She replied, "Find the most famous people you know and have them write a review of your book." I was a bit concerned because this was an obvious obstacle that I would have to overcome to finish the book. After praying, and thinking, and wondering for a few days, I remembered that I know a few notable people, but none who are famous. I reached out to them, and they all agreed. Then I remembered that I knew a person who was notable from the state of Pennsylvania. I thought, because he is not from the Detroit area, maybe this will bring a little bit of significance. So, I emailed my friend Bob.

Before I can share the rest of the story, I must tell you the extraordinary sequence of events that led me to meet Bob. It involves my friend Seth. However, we must go back, even earlier, to a time long before I met Seth. Nearly four years before I met Seth, he was in Indiana with a few friends attending a Christian retreat. During his stay at the retreat, Seth and his friends were talking about a spiritual matter, when a man walked by and offered his opinion. Bob was immediately welcomed into their conversation because he offered something new to ponder concerning their question. When the retreat ended, Bob gave his business card to Seth so they could stay in touch. More than three years later, Seth was cleaning out his garage and found a card under a bench. It was Bob's card. Seth said, "It's been so long since I have spoken to Bob. I am going to call him right now." Bob answered Seth's call. After the two of them spent a few minutes getting reacquainted, Bob invited Seth to come to Buffalo, New York for another retreat. Bob told Seth to bring some of his friends. Seth agreed.

Meanwhile, my mentor, Loren Siffring, had a memorial planned to honor his wife Rea after her passing, which I attended. While leaving the memorial, I was approached by a man that I did not know, his name was Seth. Seth informed me that he believed that God had important things for us to do together. He stated that there was a retreat coming up in Buffalo and he wanted me to come with him. I agreed to go. Seth said, "We leave in nine days."

When we arrived in Buffalo, we ended up staying at a really nice, very fancy, small hotel. It offered the intimacy of a B & B. It was quaint. This happened to be the same hotel where Bob was staying. I was introduced to Bob, who is a pastor, and we spent almost four days together on the trip. What I remembered most about Bob was that he always had his Bible in his hands, and it was always open for him to read. Fast forward, almost two and one-half years, I have written a book and I reach out to Bob to see if he will write a review for me.

Bob called me almost immediately and said he had been praying that God would send someone to his vicinity, and he believed that I was that person. On that call, Bob and I began planning a book signing tour. Bob stated, "Not only will I write a review, but I will introduce you and your book, to a friend of mine who happens to be a publisher." I was introduced to Johnny, the owner of Kingdom Publishing. He read my book and decided he wanted to publish it for me. Johnny never charged me a penny. To the surprise of both Bob and I, we would end up going out on two book tours. One of which brought us to the maple syrup factory that you read about earlier in this book.

It is moments like these, moments that could not have been made possible apart from God, that deepens your sense of *belonging*. God created me before the foundations of the earth to write a book. God made me for this.

When I was ready, God clearly told me to write my first book, "How Do I Love My Neighbor?" Along the way, He consistently made Himself known. He entwined the most amazing and remarkable circumstances to show me how much He loves me. Now you are reading the second book He asked me to write. I don't know yet in what way He will produce His magnificence. But one thing is clear, I am His! I *belong* to Him, my heavenly Father.

Stewards

1 Peter 4:10 (TPT), "Every believer has received grace gifts, so use them to serve one another as faithful stewards of the many-colored tapestry of God's grace."

Sometimes our *belonging* is revealed to us in a way that could only be believed with a faith in God. Through a series of events that only He could weave together, we finally see what we are created for. In this revealing, we clearly know who we are, and why all the struggles in our lives were necessary. Through our faithfulness, God would bring healing and acceptance and *belonging* to many. Every interaction, every trial, every tear, every sharing of His comfort only serves to further bolster our *belonging*. We take what God has given to us and share it with others so they can walk in greater wholeness. This giving of oneself, creates a happiness that cannot be explained in words, it's impossible to describe, it can only be experienced as it comes from God. I have tasted this knowledge and experienced this happiness. Nothing can compete with it as there is nothing to compare it to.

I was visiting a friend who owns a local Dairy Queen. As we were talking, a woman walked in who wanted to buy an ice cream cake. I often help those customers when I am visiting because the display freezers are in the front lobby. In this way, my friend can prevent a line from forming at the front counter. I started a conversation with the woman who was buying the cake and before long we were talking about our faith. As it turned out, we both attended the same church. Kim served on the opposite weekends as I did which is why we never saw each other before. I shared with Kim that I had a deep desire to join the Pastoral Care Team. When Kim heard this, she wore a huge smile on her face. She informed me that her husband Al was one of the current leaders of that ministry and that she lived a short distance from the Dairy Queen. Kim said that I could follow her to her house, and she would introduce me to her husband Al. While speaking with her husband, my desire to be a part of the ministry grew stronger. Al informed me that the training is six months long and is only provided once a year because of the length. The current training season was nearly completed so I would have to wait. I was excited to begin.

In the months that I waited, I was diagnosed with cancer which would hinder my ability to join the following years training session. I said to God, "God, if this ministry is where you want me, I trust that you will bring me back to it." My surgery to remove a cancerous tumor was scheduled for Monday morning. The day before, I attended church in hopes to remove the fear and anxiety I was experiencing. Many of the church members prayed over me and laid hands on me. I was still nervous. As I was getting ready to leave church and return home, one of the church officials asked me if I wanted a Stephen Minister to come to the hospital and sit with me before the surgery. Reluctantly I agreed. The next morning, I arrived at the hospital waiting room to find a man sitting with my family. I had forgotten that the church had promised to send someone. As I sat down, I asked the man, "How did you find my family in this sea of people? There must be 80 people in this waiting room." He introduced himself as Rick and said, "God knows." We sat together until the hospital called my name. I was calm because Rick was calm. He shared that God is with us in our joys and our sorrows, in the good times and the bad. We prayed together, we laughed, and we cried. When it felt appropriate, Rick excused himself. As he was walking away, I remember telling my family, "That's what I am going to do with my life." By the way, Rick and I are still entwined today.

After several months of healing, it was once again time to join the next class of potential Stephen Ministers. I was accepted into the class and after several weeks, I was paired with one of the leaders as prayer partners. This is a common practice, to have a prayer partner through training. What is unique is that I would be paired with a leader. This occurred only because there were an odd number of men in the class. When Al called me the first time, neither of us knew what would become of our relationship. Our conversations and prayers brought us closer together and closer to God. Weeks turned to months and months turned to years. Today, Al and I have been entwined for more than 15 years. We believe our relationship is 'providential.' With the benefit of Al's guidance, I completed the training and became a group facilitator in just two years. Two years later, I was invited to join the leadership team. A year after that, I was leading the group. In Pastoral Care, we always say, "The best kind of Stephen Ministers are the ones who have been on the receiving end of that kind of care. They have something tangible to give away; experience and testimony."

Being a leader is not something to take lightly. One of the most challenging responsibilities is to keep everyone encouraged and to maintain focus. Serving people is not the easiest thing to do. We must learn to listen not just to what is being said, but also what is not being said. Often, because the ministry is such a demand on our emotions and our boundaries, we have Stephen Ministers who feel the need to step away or are being called by God to different areas of ministry. Most of them are reluctant to have the departing conversation with me, probably because they don't want to let anyone down. When I know for sure that they are letting me know it's time for them to leave, I recognize I must leave them with something that I failed to offer them adequately while they were with us.

In those moments, I apologize to them. I usually say something like this, "I am sorry. Please forgive me."

Almost every time, the person I am speaking to responds with a question. They ask, "Why are you apologizing to me?"

I reply, "You think I only love you for what you can offer this ministry. I want you to know that I love you for who you are. I didn't do a good enough job conveying those thoughts to you. If I had, you would not be so reluctant to tell me it's time for you to leave. I want to thank you for serving with us in the time that you did. But I also want you to know that wherever God is calling you, that is where we want you to be. Thanks again! And remember, the door is always open if you decide to return."

Usually, the person says something like this, "I cannot tell you the weight you just lifted off my shoulders. Thank you!"

Throughout my time as one of the leaders of this ministry, there have been many returning Stephen Ministers. Why do they come back? First, they were offered the opportunity. Second, when they do come back, they bring a different intensity, almost as if they more clearly understand the calling that

God has placed on them, and the gifting that God has given them. I believe both the offering and their enlightenment through maturity speaks of their *belonging* to God. Knowing that I have the privilege of spending time with people who will allow themselves to be stretched by God to walk with hurting people in their worst seasons of life, brings such great purpose and fulfillment to me. All these moments have served to strengthen my *belonging*. To know that God is always directing our steps, doing things in the background that we are not aware of, and then to see it on full display is mind bending. However, that is what God does because we *belong* to Him. There is no way that I could have crafted this narrative, especially as it straddles so many years and utilizes all the gifts that I have been blessed with by God. I know Who I *belong* to. Hallelujah!

Paradox

Matthew 16:25 (NIV), "For whoever wants to save their life will lose it, but whoever loses their life for me will find it."

God has a way of demonstrating His goodness and providing the greatest sense of *belonging* to His children in the least likely moments. I was participating in an event that did not exist when I was a young father. My son was expecting his first child, my first grandchild, so he decided to throw what is known as a "diaper party." Most of his friends and many of the men in our family attended. All attendees, men only, were required to bring diapers for the unborn child. Not a bad way to stockpile some diapers, as they are ultra-expensive. At this party, I had a chance to catch up with many of my son's friends, some of whom I had not seen in quite some time. Dominic shared that he learned something valuable while reading my book, "How Do I Love My Neighbor."

When he brought this to my attention, I was surprised to hear that he had read my book. But after he went into greater detail as to why it was so impactful to him, God brought a sense of *belonging* than I had not previously experienced. Dominic said, "In Chapter 1, You asked the question, 'What do people see when you walk into the room?'" He continued, "I had been wanting to be more consistent in the way I dealt with my customers. I wanted to be more intentional, show more integrity, be more trustworthy. But I didn't know how to go about gaining that stature. The way you framed the question and then went about explaining it resonated with me. Thank you!"

I replied, "Dominic, I am glad that you found something valuable to add to your daily routine, and I am glad that you found that in my book." This encounter brought up a memory which immediately triggered a gentle reminder that I **belong** to God. In 2011, I was diagnosed with cancer. With a couple of operations and chemo, it appeared that I was healthy. However, at the four and one-half-year mark, the cancer came back. As a result, another surgery was scheduled with the same oncologist who performed the first surgery. The week prior to the surgery, the oncologist called me and informed me that due to circumstances beyond his control not only was he leaving the medical system that my insurance had recognized, but that he was unable to perform the surgery. He did encourage me with the notion that the hospital would be calling me with an action plan to proceed. The hospital did call me the next day to inform me that they did have a surgeon who was ready to step in and deliver the treatment necessary during surgery.

The following Monday, I checked in for surgery as scheduled. After the medical staff prepared me for surgery, I waited in the pre-op area for the surgeon to arrive. My wife was on the right side of the bed and Bill, my prayer team leader, was on the left side when the surgeon arrived. He introduced himself and then assured me that he was qualified to step in and informed of the intimate details of my situation. It was then that he shared the news that I was unprepared to hear. He stated that he does not paint "Norman Rockwell" pictures for his patients. He said that he always wants his patients to be informed about the severity of their circumstances. Therefore, he needed me to know that one of my vocal cords would die in the surgery and he would do his best to preserve the other. He said that when I wake up from the surgery, the best scenario is that I would be hoarse for the rest of my life, but that there was also a strong possibility that I would never speak again. My wife, my prayer team leader, and I prayed for Gods protection and favor and then I was wheeled into surgery.

When I woke from surgery, I was informed that the surgeon never touched my vocal cords, and that the surgery was a complete success. Praise God! After more chemo treatments and time to heal, I finally made it to the five-year threshold when the medical community considers a person in remission. It was my conversation with Dominic that spurred this memory and the realization that in God's kingdom there are many examples of the *paradox* (two opposing truths that occupy the same space). We see unseen things; we conquer by yielding; we find rest under a yoke; we reign by serving; we are made great by becoming small; we are exalted when we are humble; we become wise by being fools for Christ's sake; we are made free by becoming bondservants; we gain strength when we are weak; we triumph through defeat; we find victory by glorying in our illnesses; we live by dying; we find our life by losing it; the impossible is possible with Jesus.

Even if I could not speak verbally, God had already provided a way for me to speak despite the cancer. Long before I ever dreamt of writing a book, God had already planted in me the ability to speak through written words.

Psalm 139:13-18 (NIV), "For you created my inmost being; you knit me together in my mother's womb. I praise you because I am fearfully and wonderfully made; your works are wonderful, I know that full well. My frame was not hidden from you when I was made in the secret place, when I was woven together in the depths of the earth. Your eyes saw my unformed body; all the days ordained for me were written in your book before one of them came to be. How precious to me are your thoughts, God! How vast is the sum of them! Were I to count them, they would outnumber the grains of sand—when I awake, I am still with you."

Only after an unlikely conversation, years later, was I able to see what once was hidden. God continues to reveal Himself and I am constantly reminded that I **belong** to Him. By the way, a few days after this encounter, God revealed the title of the next book He wants me to write, "Eyes That See." I don't know when He will ask me to begin writing. For now, He has provided the title and that is enough. When He tells me to begin writing, I will obey.

Immeasurable

Ephesians 3:20-21 (NIV), "Now to him who is able to do immeasurably more than all we ask or imagine, according to his power that is at work within us, to him be glory in the church and in Christ Jesus throughout all generations, for ever and ever! Amen."

When I was still a very young Christian, I remember when the yearning of wanting something more became a cry for help. I didn't understand it in that moment, but I was finally ready to surrender my life to God. I didn't know what that was going to look like, but I knew that I was still missing something. Fulfillment, contentment, purpose, joy, peace, and to some degree, gratitude were all absent from my life. I was traveling once again for work and away from home. I reached the point when I knew I could not muster any more than what I had already established on my own. The newness of my faith had carried me only so far. I needed more. What I was about to do was enter into a relationship with the God who woke me from my slumber. The God who created me with great purpose, the God who knit me together in my mother's womb, the One who would show me the mystery, Christ, the hope of glory would draw me closer and closer unto Him. All I knew in those moments was that what I had been doing wasn't enough.

While working away from home, I was staying in a run-down hotel. I felt like there was no end to the emptiness that I was experiencing. I was walking into these auto plants each day and wondering what the result was. Did anyone's life change because of what I was doing? Each morning I walked into these buildings, and it was still dark outside. When I left in the evening, it was dark outside. Almost all these buildings are absent of windows, so daylight is rarely seen. I found myself in this endless cycle. Three nights in a row I cried out to the Lord from my hotel room. I remember the anguish and the tears. I would read His Word and cry out, almost to the point of screaming, "God! There has to be more to life than this!" I wanted desperately to hear from Him. I needed direction. I needed hope. I needed Him to prepare a way. Then on the third night, He clearly told me that I would have a new job in a year. His message was so valuable, it was life giving. With newfound hope, I was ready to face my monotonous, gloomy existence again. The journey that followed was not at all what I expected. Many stops along the way created more confusion than clarity. My life changed in ways that I could have never imagined.

Shortly after God spoke to me, I was laid off from my job. A few months later, my wife would be diagnosed with cancer and need chemotherapy and surgery. I started wondering, "Where was God?" Looking back on that season, I was able to meet all my wife's needs. I could take her to all her doctor appointments, chemo sessions, and provide care for her when she returned home from surgery. When my wife and I had a chance to look back, we could finally see God's provision during that season. Soon after, I was able to start my own company. For five years, I walked in and out of people's homes performing basic handyman services and sharing the love of Christ. I thought those were the best years I had ever seen. I thought, "How could life get any better?" When cancer struck me and I was forced to liquidate everything, I was confused. Somehow life got better. When cancer struck me a second time, I didn't know what to think, but I knew God was with me. Once again, life got better. I became a chaplain and a pastor and began to serve God in a greater capacity. Life got better! Happiness, fulfillment, and *belonging* were solidified more and more. Then came the most horrific blow of my life, my son Michael died. Once again, God made His presence known and *belonging* was more fully established.

I cried out to the Lord, and He answered me.

I thought I might be able to plot my course and clearly see what He would do with me. However, from the onset, He did things that I was not prepared for. I experienced things that I never expected. I had to learn to trust Him. I asked Him to be my Lord, and that required my surrender.

People have often asked, "If you had to do it all over again, what part would you change?" That is a very difficult question to ponder. Of course, there are things that I would never have asked to endure. If I were to change one thing, would I have the perspective that I now have? The circumstances of my life, in its entirety, have provided the lens from which I can see God in clear detail. I know without question that I *belong* to Him. He has proven Himself time and time again. My life is full and my lack is gone because He made it so. My Heavenly Father loves me, and He created me to walk with Him. There isn't a single element of my life that He has not leveraged to bring about healing, friendship, love, and *belonging*.

-Lessons Learned-

What Christ has done in and through my life is nothing short of miraculous. Every hurt, every sorrow, every broken moment He has turned into a blessing. In the most remarkable way, my life has been refined, redeemed, and restored. I implore you to give God your life with no reservations and watch what He does. Along the journey, He will help you realize that you **belong** to Him. It will be uncomfortable to say the least. However, He will utilize every aspect of your life to bring Him glory if you allow Him to. Life giving hope comes when we can share our experiences with others. We can never know who we may touch with our story, but the message is clear: "See, God brought me through it. He can do the same for you."

Salvation Prayer

There's a chance that not everyone who reads this book knows Jesus. For those who have yet to ask Jesus into your heart as Lord and Savior and receive the gift of salvation, please read this prayer, and be filled with the Holy Spirit. You may not know it yet, but soon enough you will realize that you ***belong*** to Jesus!

Lord Jesus, for too long I've kept you out of my life. I know that I am a sinner and that I cannot save myself. No longer will I close the door when I hear you knocking. By faith I gratefully receive your gift of salvation. I am ready to trust you as my Lord and Savior. Thank you, Lord Jesus, for coming to earth. I believe you are the Son of God who died on the cross for my sins and rose from the dead on the third day. Thank you for bearing my sins and giving me the gift of eternal life. I believe your words are true. Come into my heart, Lord Jesus, and be my Savior. Fill me with Your Holy Spirit. Amen.

Romans 10:9-10 (NIV), 'If you declare with your mouth, "Jesus is Lord," and believe in your heart that God raised him from the dead, you will be saved. For it is with your heart that you believe and are justified, and it is with your mouth that you profess your faith and are saved.'

The dignity of serving God is second only to the dignity of belonging to His family. (Author Unknown)

Afterword

Jackson,

Love is a verb, and when properly bestowed, it continually apprehends its receiver. Recipients of love can be renewed every day with an undergirding of freshness, bringing awareness of value, and a deeper sense of **belonging**. I pray the love you receive transforms you moment by moment. I pray you never experience a lack of love, but always live in the abundance of it. I pray you one day meet the Lord Jesus Christ, if you don't know Him, because He can take the love you have received and multiply it beyond comprehension and constantly reinforce your **belonging**.

1 Corinthians 13 (NIV), "If I speak in the tongues of men or of angels, but do not have love, I am only a resounding gong or a clanging cymbal. If I have the gift of prophecy and can fathom all mysteries and all knowledge, and if I have a faith that can move mountains, but do not have love, I am nothing. If I give all I possess to the poor and give over my body to hardship that I may boast, but do not have love, I gain nothing. Love is patient, love is kind. It does not envy, it does not boast, it is not proud. It does not dishonor others, it is not self-seeking, it is not easily angered, it keeps no record of wrongs. Love does not delight in evil but rejoices with the truth. It always protects, always trusts, always hopes, always perseveres. Love never fails. But where there are prophecies, they will cease; where there are tongues, they will be stilled; where there is knowledge, it will pass away. For we know in part and we prophesy in part, but when completeness comes, what is in part disappears. When I was a child, I talked like a child, I thought like a child, I reasoned like a child. When I became a man, I put the ways of childhood behind me. For now we see only a reflection as in a mirror; then we shall see face to face. Now I know in part; then I shall know fully, even as I am fully known. And now these three remain: faith, hope and love. But the greatest of these is love.

Jeff Frick

Scripture References

Dedication
Numbers 6:24-26

Acknowledgments
1 Thessalonians 1:2

Author's Note
1 Peter 2:9

Chapter Break
Psalm 100:3

Chapter 1
John 1:12
Romans 12:4-5
Colossians 1:15-17
Genesis 1:26-27
Hebrews 4:15
James 4:7
Acts 20:28
Psalm 27:10
Philippians 4:8
Psalm 34:8
Ephesians 1:3-5
Romans 12:9
Ephesians 6:18

Chapter 2
Genesis 11:4-6
Matthew 21:9
Galatians 2:11-21
James 3:17
Romans 16:17
1 Timothy 4:1-3
Proverbs 25:26

2 Corinthians 6:14
James 4:4
John 17:20-23
1 Corinthians 1:10
Ephesians 4:1-6

Chapter 3
Psalm 42:3
2 Corinthians 1:3-4
Colossians 1:20
Martha Hickman, Healing after Loss (HarperCollins Publishers Inc, 1994)
July 7
Psalm 23:6
Psalm 13:1-2
Hebrews 13:2
1 Corinthians 9:19-23

Chapter 4
Psalm 119:82
James 2:8-9
Colossians 3:21
James 3:9-10
Romans 5:5
Proverbs 17:17
Chapter Break
Psalm 24:1

Chapter 5
Romans 2:1-5
Ecclesiastes 1:18
Psalm 91:1-6
James 4:17
Romans 15:5-7
Proverbs 14:29
Micah 6:8
Galatians 3:24-29
2 Corinthians 3:14
Isaiah 64:6
John 16:33

Psalm 107:2-3

Chapter 6
1 John 2:15
James 1:22-25
Watchman Nee, Spiritual Authority (Christian Fellowship Publishers Inc, 1972) Pg. 21
Matthew 6:19-21
Proverbs 11:2
Psalm 100
Philippians 1:6
Hosea 3:1
Colossians 3:14
Eugene Peterson, Working the Angles (Wm. B. Eerdmans Publishers Co., 1987) Chp. 9
Isaiah 40:31
Hebrews 13:7
Romans 8:28
1 Corinthians 3:23

Chapter 7
Matthew7:7-8
Luke 3:5
Acts 24:16
Hebrews 13:18
Colossians 1:27-29
Romans 5:6
Now I Belong to Jesus, lyrics & music by Norman J Clayton
Philippians 4:6-7
1 Corinthians 16:22
Psalm 32:8
John 2:1-11
Matthew 19:26
1 Peter 4:10
Matthew 16:25
Psalm 139:13-18
Ephesians 3:20-21

Salvation Prayer
Romans 10:9-10

Afterword
1 Corinthians 13

Other Books by
Jeff

How Do I Love my Neighbor? 4 Promises and 6 Truths available on Amazon

Jeff Frick

Property of GRAM Ministry

GRAM Ministry
48366 Whatley Court
Shelby Township, MI 48315
248.431.4051
Gramministry@gmail.com
Gramministry.org

About The Author

Jeff is a pastor, chaplain, teacher, mentor, pastoral care provider and an author. He lives with his wife Laura in Shelby Township, Michigan, and they have been married for more than 30 years. He is a father, a grandfather, a brother, a son, and a friend to many. He has served in various organizations over the years in the community in which he lives. Jeff is involved in discipling men in several churches, and currently has a home-based fellowship in Shelby Township where he serves as a pastor.

Jeff's passions include reading, writing, teaching, mentoring, counseling, and discipling men. He is a life-long learner and shares his knowledge with the dozens he counsels and serves. He is also founder/president of GRAM (**G**od **R**efines **A**ll **M**en, **G**od **R**edeems **A**ll **M**en, **G**od **R**estores **A**ll **M**en) Ministry. His ministry, of nearly two decades, has primarily been in small groups and one-on-one encounters.

Many long-established spiritual leaders have poured into Jeff over the years. He believes this spiritual capital God has poured into him should be invested into the lives of others. Jeff spends his days encouraging men to receive the grace of our Father in Heaven and to trust Jesus, His Son, as their life source and purpose.

Printed in the USA
CPSIA information can be obtained
at www.ICGtesting.com
CBHW051705031223
2322CB00003B/11